CRYSTAL PROSPERITY

CRYSTAL PROSPERITY

Create abundance
in all areas of your life

JUDY HALL

METRO BOOKS
NEW YORK

Picture Credits: **Alamy**/Greg C Grace: 127T; WILDLIFE
GmbH: 48, 101T, 140. **Getty Images**/Dorling Kindersley:
108C, 126T, 128. **Karen Hatch**: 7. **Ivan Hissey**: 11, 25,
51, 55, 64, 75, 83, 97, 99, 125. **iStockphoto.com**: 3, 12,
21, 46, 62, 63, 133, 155; Stacy Able: 130; Arpad Benedek:
68B, 78, 79, 94T, 101B, 145B; Sun Chan: 144B; Cindy
England: 58; Donald Erickson: 22, 34; Umut Ersah: 139B;
Christoph Hähnel: 111; Robert Kacpura: 31; Danish Khan:
131B; Martin Novak: 82, 86T, 90; Raigorodski Pavel: 31,
66L, 148C; Stuart Pitkin: 17; Dave White: 15, 89. **Andrew
Perris**: 1, 26, 37, 41, 42, 45, 61, 67L, 93, 102B, 104B,
106C, 110T, 113T, 120T, 120C, 122T, 122B, 134, 135,
136T, 138T, 147B, 150B, 153B. **Photos.com**, a division
of Getty Images: 5, 18, 19, 32, 38, 38, 72, 86B, 131T, 160.

Metro books
122 Fifth Avenue
New York, NY 10011

ISBN: 978-1-4351-2301-4

Printed and bound in China

10 9 8 7 6 5 4 3 2 1

This book was conceived, designed, and produced by
Leaping Hare Press
210 High Street, Lewes
East Sussex BN7 2NS, UK
www.leapingharepress.co.uk

Creative Director Peter Bridgewater
Publisher Debbie Thorpe
Art Director Wayne Blades
Senior Editor Polita Anderson
Designer Sarah Howerd

Disclaimer The rituals and layouts in this book do not
constitute financial advice nor do they guarantee rapid
success. Your prosperity depends on how well aligned
your inner and outer intentions are, and how positively
focused you remain. Only you can achieve this.
Nevertheless, it is sincerely hoped that the book
contributes to your becoming enriched in every way.

Contents

Author Profile _____ 6–7

Introduction _____ 8–9

Chapter 1
What is Prosperity? _____ 10

Chapter 2
Crystal Tools _____ 50

Chapter 3
Crystals for Specific Outcomes _____ 98

Chapter 4
The Prosperity Stones Directory _____ 124

Index _____ 156

Further Reading and Acknowledgments _____ 160

Judy Hall is an internationally known crystal facilitator and author who lives in the UK. Her Crystal Bibles are the best-selling crystal books in the USA and UK; Volume 1 has been translated into more than ten languages and sold over a million copies. Her other books include Crystal Healing, The Crystal Zodiac, Psychic Self-Protection: using crystals to change your life, and Crystal Experience: a workshop in a book. Judy runs crystal, astrological, and psychic protection workshops for all levels of experience, and works with people from around the world.

Fascinated with crystals and stones since she was a child, Judy remembers using crystals to heal and generate energy in her previous lives, a skill that she has instinctively drawn on in her present life. Her lifelong interest in the history of stones and curiosity as to how their properties were first identified led her to study for a Masters Degree in Cultural Astronomy and Astrology, in which she examined connections between the sky, gods, planets, stones, and healing practices across many ancient cultures. Judy has been using crystals in her healing and astrological work for more than thirty-five years and created the exercises in this book to ensure her own crystal prosperity and that of her clients.

7

Introduction

Crystal Prosperity

Prosperity is a hot topic during uncertain times, which tend to focus attention on money, or lack of it. We worry about future prospects, our ability to support ourselves, keep a job, provide for our old age, attract abundance, and so on—although there are many suggestions as to how this can be done. Maybe you enthusiastically took up "cosmic ordering"—asking the universe for what you want—only to find it hasn't yet delivered and you're beginning to feel cheated or to wonder what else you can do.

From my point of view, we would be much better employed in generating prosperity for ourselves and using our power of intent to enrich our lives. In attracting abundance on all levels and creating an unshakable sense of well-being and inner enrichment, we are truly wealthy. This doesn't mean being relentlessly positive; you need to examine your underlying beliefs and acknowledge doubts and fears and then transmute, rather than deny, them. But you always have the choice of taking the positive view.

Crystals have been used for thousands of years as a means to attract prosperity, yet until now there haven't been any books published on crystals for wealth, prosperity, and abundance. This book looks at what prosperity is and how to attract abundance of all kinds into your life with the aid of crystals. I know from a lifetime of working with crystals that they amplify, potentize, and manifest our deepest desires and act as powerful attractors. This book shares how you, too, can create crystal prosperity for yourself. You'll discover what works best for you and how you personally are going to interact with the magic of crystals. This is a richness you then take into any area of your life.

Crystal Prosperity is not just a book about attracting money into your life; it shows you how to create a real sense of abundance and well-being. It helps you to enhance and build upon previous work. Maybe you're already beginning to recognize that it may be more beneficial to find an inner sense of security that is not dependent on outer circumstances. Pointing out that there are many ways of being wealthy, *Crystal Prosperity* examines what enriches life in addition to money, encompassing skills, gifts, relationships, and home–work balance. Merely reading the book won't enrich your life. Doing the exercises and taking a hard look at what you believe about prosperity will. Keeping a journal helps you to track those changes and to appreciate your enriched life.

Judy Hall

Citrine

Chapter 1

What is Prosperity?

It is our attitude to prosperity that determines how much abundance we enjoy and whether we live a fundamentally enriched life. Holocaust survivor Victor Frankl lost his whole family, all his possessions, and many of his friends, but said: "Everything can be taken away from a man but one thing—to choose one's attitude in a given set of circumstances, to choose one's own way." This insight enriched his life.

In this chapter, we look at what true prosperity is, what it means to you, and how to work with it to create a real sense of abundance and well-being now—and how to attract prosperity of all kinds into your life. Exploring what enriches life, this chapter examines many ways of being wealthy that do not rely on how much money you have in the bank. The tools include visualizations, affirmations, rituals, and layouts using prosperity crystals. You explore your deepest attitudes to wealth, and discover how you can use the magic of crystals to enrich all areas of your life.

Crystal Prosperity

Conceived in the womb of the earth, *diamonds, rubies, sapphires, and emeralds are the most precious of gems. These gifts of an abundant universe have always been worn to signify wealth and status. Not all crystals are bright and shining. Many are dull and grainy—you wouldn't value them unless you were attuned to their amazing properties.*

BELOW: Deep blue with golden inclusions of pyrites, which shimmer like little stars, Lapis Lazuli resembles the night sky.

It may surprise you to know that you already use crystals. They power watches, microchips, and lasers; act as spark plugs; and minerals form the basis of many medicines. Crystals have always been used for adornment, and people have forgotten why they were worn in the first place. This was not merely for beauty, as ancient texts show. Many of the stones are semiprecious—opaque chunks of rock. Some of these ancient treasures resemble the night sky (Lapis Lazuli) or glow bright red like lifeblood (Carnelian). To early cultures, the properties of crystals were clearly more important than appearance. Texts and grave goods show the Babylonians and Egyptians associated stones with their gods and recognized specific healing, protective, and manifestation properties. Stones have been used for these purposes ever since, imbuing them with even more potency. Due to translation problems, we no longer know

12

what Maziuquez is, but we know it assisted in holding onto your possessions in ancient Mesopotamia, Arabia, and medieval Spain. The thirteenth-century Spanish *Lapidary of King Alfonso X the Learned* tells us so. However, we can use other crystals that have an equally long history.

So What Do Crystals Do?

Crystals generate, conserve, radiate, and amplify energy. Holding Quartz triples the bioenergy field around your body. This energy amplification is one of the reasons we instinctively feel good when we hold a crystal that is in tune with our own vibrations. Due to the way the internal crystalline structure of a stone is arranged—its lattice— energy moves slowly or rapidly through the stone or may become trapped within it. Many crystals have a powerful infusion of minerals within their matrix and, as doctors will tell you, minerals have a specific effect on the human body.

Crystals create prosperity by taking your personal intention, potentizing, amplifying, and sending it out into the universe to attract back all that you wish for. In other words, they appear to work magic, but the true source is the extraordinary power of your own thoughts and the attractor factor—of which we hear more shortly.

13

Prosperity Consciousness

Crystal Prosperity

Prosperity is a state of mind and a way of well-being. It is more than having money and possessions, although naturally these have their place. Prosperity consciousness is about feeling satisfied and secure with what you have, living an enriching and fulfilling life, sharing life's bounty, feeling gratitude, and trusting that the universe provides appropriately for your needs.

If you are struggling with money issues, and especially if you feel stuck in a poverty trap, this definition of prosperity may sound like claptrap. As may the statement that, to a large extent, we create what we experience. But think about it. Many people put all their attention on hard times to come, and wonder why those times quickly manifest, or they bemoan the fact that hard times are here and wonder why they stay. They feel that the world owes them a living yet do nothing to create a space where prosperity flourishes, or they believe they are a victim of circumstances they cannot change.

There are people who grasp an opportunity when it presents itself, no matter how cunningly it is packaged or how much it might look like a disaster. During a recession in the 1980s, it was impossible to find a window cleaner in the small town in the UK where I was living. Then, one day, a guy leafleted the town offering window-cleaning services. He'd been laid off from a high-powered job. His wife had said: "Well, if you've nothing else to do, get the ladder out and clean the windows, I can't get a window cleaner for love nor money." So, he thought, if she needs a window cleaner, so do other people. Hence, the leaflet drop. After a few months he was earning more than before and spending more time with his family. He thoroughly enjoyed meeting people and could choose his own hours. After the recession was over, he decided not to go back to his old career. When asked what made him truly happy, he said, "self-respect." He didn't measure his worth by what he did or how other people might view his occupation, but by who he was as a person. If you have self-respect, you never feel demeaned by a job or what other people think of you, as we will see.

Think about your own attitude for a moment. Do you believe that prosperity is all about having money and financial success—and that your world will fall apart if you lose a job or don't achieve your monetary ambitions? Some people—and you may be one of them at this moment—fantasize about the difference having

BELOW: Green Aventurine can reinforce decisiveness, and can help us to see other alternatives, gently encouraging us to persevere.

15

unlimited money would make, the happiness it would bring, how different life would be. Desire for money literally rules some people's lives. If they have money, they want more, and more, and yet are never satisfied.

Ask yourself, do you judge your worth—and that of others—by job, status, or wealth. Do you feel demeaned if your job is not "good enough," rather than seeing your role as a valuable contribution to society? Your inner attitude makes an enormous difference. To someone who feels impoverished, the world invariably looks bleak. To someone who feels powerless, it seems that someone else is in control. Ask yourself, do you feel like a victim of circumstances? If you do, you are unlikely to view your life as fulfilling and will experience an inner poverty rather than a sense of living a rich life.

But it doesn't have to be like this. True prosperity comes from an inner contentment and generosity of spirit that naturally attracts wealth of all kinds. It comes from the richness of friends, a good work-leisure balance, and a healthy attitude to money. And it most certainly comes from trusting that we live in an abundant universe. This doesn't mean pretending that everything's okay, or denying that there are problems.

We need to be honest with ourselves. Negative feelings can be useful warnings to us—but you don't have to stay entrenched in them or feel them every day. Nor do you have to deny how you are feeling and pretend to be positive. There is a huge difference between being realistically positive when assessing possibilities and adopting an unrealistic Pollyanna approach that takes no account of actualities, such as bills piling up. If you continually assert that things will go wrong, they inevitably do. But if you look at what could feasibly go wrong and plan a way through to the other side, setting realistic goals and trusting the process, good things manifest.

Throughout this book we look at many different manifestations of richness in life and you learn how to tune into these for yourself. We explore the attitudes of mind and core beliefs that hold you back, the fears, self-pity, and negative self-talk that get in the way, and you learn how to surrender to the process of prosperity.

BELOW: Clear Quartz generates energy while Amethyst aids creative thinking and spiritual awareness.

Start with one small step If you are in the habit of filling the space after an amount on a check with a line, desist. Allow the amount to fly free with no limitation. See it as the start of abundance.

Looking within your own self is the secret of finding true abundance: cashing in on your own resources. You have all the riches and resources you need within yourself to create an abundant world. You just need to believe it. And to tap into your inner world you need the power of intention and sufficient impetus to take those first small steps.

BELOW: Jade can promote courage and self-sufficiency, helping to balance the emotions.

It's all very well, you may be saying at this point, but I'm unemployed or in a low-paid job, or I've lost everything or am in danger of doing so and none of it's my fault. In other words, you may be feeling sorry for yourself rather than having compassion for the place you find yourself in. To "poor me," the world looks bleak. You appear to lack resources and, as a result, you abandon hope. If you don't feel rich, it is all too easy to feel apathetic, powerless, and helpless, and it has been shown that apathy equals poverty, despair, and hopelessness. This "poor me" attitude creates a vicious circle that can be broken by the exercises, visualizations, rituals, and layouts that follow. As long as your life feels secure and inwardly enriched, you wait with equanimity for abundance to manifest.

The Steps to Abundance

- Changing your mental program—what your mind conceives, it achieves.

- Measuring your self-worth by who you are, not what you do or what you have.

- Following your bliss—do what you love and abundance follows.

- Obeying the fundamental law of attraction—like follows like.

- Believing you can fulfill your dreams.

- Noticing and appreciating all the small joys of everyday life.

- Recognizing that the universe wants you to succeed.

- Focusing on exactly what you want to attract right now.

- Giving yourself time, kindness, and compassion.

- Avoiding doubt and guilt and no longer procrastinating.

- Letting go of fear or self-pity.

- Sharing what you have and taking pleasure in giving.

BELOW: Jade has long been regarded as a stone of the highest value and can generate abundance and serenity.

Take a small step now Ask yourself what is your most enriching quality. Go out and share it with someone right now.

19

Crystal Prosperity

Like attracts like. *Ask yourself whether you are an attractor or a repeller? Do you attract good fortune or push it away? Do you let in the good stuff or shut off the flow? The choice is yours. The biggest contribution you can make right now to your ability to attract prosperity is to monitor your thoughts and look at what you believe deep down inside yourself, because this is what creates your world.*

"Why would anyone push good fortune away?" you may ask. But we all do it from time to time, simply by the way we think and what we believe. If your core beliefs are negative or if they deny what you really want, change them! Remember that like attracts like, and opposites repel. If you have a constant litany of negative thoughts running through your head, transform it. Focus on feeling enriched and believe that you create what you need. Start attracting all the good things of life to you, not just money. By releasing our self-limiting beliefs, leaving behind the conditioning of childhood and culture, we align to a totally different energetic blueprint. What you talk about and put your thoughts on, manifests. So, start thinking about prosperity and joy and you'll have them in abundance.

20

The desire for money, or for more, more, more, rules many people's lives. As a result, they never feel like there is enough. They never feel satisfied. All the energy goes into accumulation and greed, to feed that insatiable itch for more. If the purpose of life is financial success and that eludes you, what then? Life is empty, or appears that way. When you feel barren, what you attract to yourself is even more barrenness to bolster that feeling of there not being enough. If you start to feel gratitude for what you have rather than demanding "more!," you create a space in which more manifests.

And remember that you may not get quite what you visualize. What you ask for may manifest in a different way because that is what you need to enrich your life fully.

BELOW: By integrating items with special meaning to you, you can enhance the energy of your personal space.

Take a small step now Create an altar—not an altar to money, but rather a sacred space that encourages prosperity to manifest in your life. Put pictures and items that symbolize not only what you want to attract into your life, but all the good things that already enrich your life and for which you are thankful.

How Do I Feel About Money?

Beliefs surrounding prosperity have an enormous bearing on the amount of money you attract into your life. How you feel about money determines what you do with it, how and what you spend it on, the pleasure you get out of it, how long it stays with you—and even whether it comes to you in the first place. So often what underpin your feelings are cultural and family mindsets.

First, notice how you feel about the statement—what you really believe about money. Does money excite and inspire you, or does it feel uncomfortable even thinking about it? Does thinking about money immediately depress you because you lack money and can't see that you'll ever have any? Do you spend hours in fruitless imaginings based on "when I win the lottery" and so on? Do you hoard money "in case" and live a fundamentally impoverished life in the meantime? For some people, money is one asset among many, something one either has or doesn't have, but it's not particularly important. For other people, and indeed some cultures, money is all there is. It's how they measure status. It's the basis of their self-worth and how they assess themselves against other people. If they lose their money, they feel like they've lost everything. Let's look at why that might be.

BELOW: Agate is a soothing, calming crystal that encourages you to take a step back from your problems, helping you to regain balance in your life.

22

Have you ever been told that life is a struggle, you have
to work hard for what you get, the economy is failing so
it's all downhill from here, and you'll never be able to
afford that to which you aspire? Was there a message in
your childhood that rich people are greedy and there is
virtue in poverty, or the opposite, "easy come, easy go,
there's always tomorrow." Deep down inside do you
believe that the world owes you a living, that you have
to be practical, that there's no room for dreams; or that
there isn't enough to go round, that someone has to
suffer or do the dirty jobs in life, or that the only job
worth having is one with security and "prospects."
Were you taught that the spiritual path and money don't
go together, or that "people like us don't have jobs like
that"? Were you told that it's selfish to want things for
yourself and that money is the root of all evil? Many of
us were unknowingly programmed with toxic thoughts
like this from a young age, and many of those thoughts
become excuses or substitutes for generating money. If
you believe any of the above statements, you are unlikely
to feel inwardly prosperous or to have a healthy attitude
toward money. Toxic views such as these lead to poverty
and not to prosperity consciousness.

23

Ask Yourself

If someone gave you a million dollars right now, what you would do with it? Would you instantly pay off your mortgage, put it in the bank for a rainy day, go out and blow the lot, or, as someone I knew said: "give it to the charity that drills water wells for Africa." Take a few minutes to write down everything that comes to mind. It could tell you a great deal about what you really feel and believe about money.

The woman who responded with "Water Aid" was living an outwardly prosperous middle-class life in a beautiful house, but her husband was struggling to pay the mortgage despite his high salary. She dressed in hand-me-downs "to save money." It was as though by behaving as if they were poor and by struggling, they "paid" for living in the beautiful home, and that somehow made it acceptable to her.

When she examined her response, she realized that she'd been taught in childhood that charity was what mattered. Her parents' view was that if you had "spare" money, you should give it to the poor and needy. Money wasn't something to be enjoyed, nor to provide more than the basic necessities in your life—a classic case of poverty consciousness. Even though her parents were comfortably off, they lived a miserly life and, paradoxically, saved hard "just in case." As so often happens, the "just in case" did materialize and all their money went on care in their old age so there was nothing for the daughter to inherit. With the assistance of Green Calcite, the woman began to ask herself whether this was really how she felt. She soon realized that although she'd been saying that the universe was abundant and that all would be well, she hadn't behaved like that. She had unconsciously lived out her parents' pattern. So, she changed her attitude to money. There wasn't any more money in her life, but she felt enriched by what she had. Somehow, there was always enough. To ask yourself more questions about your attitude to money, turn to pages 80–85.

RIGHT: You don't need to wait for any conditions to change in order to be conscious of abundance. This universe is waiting to fulfill your every need.

25

What Do I Value?

You are your greatest asset.

So, do you value yourself? Do you give yourself the love, respect, validation, and compassion that you deserve? Do you feel enriched by knowing yourself in all your complexity and beauty? Do you like being you? And do you value other things that lack monetary worth but that enrich your life? What you value has a powerful effect on how you spend your life. Do you value friendship and the company of like-minded people, the joy of sharing time with those you love?

You probably value what you were brought up to believe was valuable, and you are rich, indeed, if you were taught to value not only your true self but also nature and beauty and joy. If you weren't, there's no time like the present to take a look at all the wondrous things around you.

"The poor" aren't just those people who are financially deprived. "The poor" include people who lack communication skills, have low expectations, and a poor sense of their own worth. People who are impoverished in this way tend to value only things that are money-based and particularly anything that can buy a few moments of forgetfulness. What is rare is a sense of well-being. To get out of a poverty trap, a fundamental change in values is

BELOW: Smoky Quartz is a gentle, grounding stone that can enhance quiet reflection during meditation.

26

needed—and a change in focus. Watching a magnificent sunset is a deeply enriching experience, as are a few moments of silent communication or contributing to society. It all depends on what you value. Simply taking time to be yourself can be the most enriching thing of all. So, ask yourself what you really value and how much time you give to the things that truly matter in your life.

Exercise

Write down ten people you admire and why you admire them, the qualities that give them value in your eyes. Try to recognize that quality in yourself.

Make a list of the twenty things you value most in life. How many of these are free? Did your list include yourself?

People who take time out of their day for quiet communion with themselves or their god—in other words, for meditation or prayer—have an inner resource of deep peace and contentment that serves them well on their journey through life. The Dalai Lama says that, if he is exceptionally busy, he gets up even earlier to fit in an extra hour's meditation. If you lack time, meditation can be fitted into your journey to work (assuming you're not

How Much Value Do I Give to My Time?

Time can be a precious commodity in these pressured times.
If you are oveburdening yourself with work, running to a standstill,
ask yourself:

How much of my time is filled with things I value and how much with things
that have to be done to make money?

Could I downshift without losing my sense of worth? (If not, see pages 30–33)

Would a smaller house, less material goods, and more time spent playing with
my children, being with my partner, or simply walking the dog be beneficial?

Could I find time to meditate for fifteen minutes each day?

Could I delegate or drop many of the things that make me feel so pressured?

Could I find time to be mindful of all the things around me that could give me
joy if only I noticed them?

Could I donate a portion of my time to help others?

What, in how I spend my time, do I value most of all?

driving), or you can do it last thing at night as a quiet wind down before bed. You don't have to sit still to meditate though. Try a fifteen-minute walking mindfulness meditation in your lunch hour in which you simply notice, and have gratitude for, all the little things around you: the child at play, the beauty of a bird, the shape of a cloud, the color of the sky, or the lusciousness a flower; the sounds, the smells, and the rich variety of people you pass by.

Valuing My Work

Some people feel that they have to apologize for what they do, for the job that they have become stuck in, or indeed for lack of a job. It adds immeasurably to your sense of worth if what you value is the contribution you make to society and to your own well-being through working.

Questions to Ponder

Do I value myself? Am I my most potent and valuable asset?

Do I find time to do the things I enjoy simply for pleasure? If not, why not?

Crystal Prosperity

Being who you intrinsically are rather than who or what you—or anyone else—think you should be or become is crucial if you are to value yourself and live an enriched life. Self-esteem, self-respect, and self-worth are the basis of your inner wealth. Your self-esteem should not rest on how much money you have or in what you own or what other people think of you but in who you are as a person. Living in alignment with your deepest beliefs makes you wealthy.

Low self-esteem is indicated by the need for external validation, the good opinion of others, status symbols, and trappings of success: the fast car, big house, social acceptance, and trophy wife or husband or its equivalent. It's shown by a desperate need to prove yourself, or an insatiable greed for approval and a desire to win at all costs. It's signaled by deep dissatisfaction with yourself, constantly thinking you need to be "better," and a tendency to please others or adjust your views to reflect those of people you consider to be more important than yourself. It's about an unconscious lack within yourself that drives you to seek in another what is missing in yourself instead of recognizing it within yourself. The biggest barrier to prosperity is that, in many cultures,

we are taught to value ourselves for what we achieve in
the external world or how we fit into the idea someone
else has of us. This is often accompanied by the view
that the individual must subsume his or her needs for
the good of the whole. But this is not so! Abundance
is all about appreciating and valuing yourself exactly as
you are right now. Having an unshakable sense of your
own inner worth is one of the richest resources you have.
So how do you get it?

* Start being you
* The you who is here right now
* Manifest who you truly are

BELOW: Lapis Lazuli
is a powerful stone
for those seeking
spiritual development;
it promotes serenity
and self-acceptance.

Build up your sense of worth a step at a time. Each time
you waver, tell yourself you have equal value to everyone
else. It's not about what you do but rather about who you
are. Nevertheless, what you achieve can be a foundation
for self-worth. Make a point of noticing all the little
things you do—and set sensible goals that you can easily
achieve rather than shooting for the moon. Each
time you achieve something, each task that you
fulfill, each goal you reach successfully, each

good day you have, pat yourself on the back. Give yourself a treat (remembering that treats do not need to center around money). Don't berate yourself for not doing more. Respect yourself for what you have achieved rather than for what you have not yet done. Be as kind and compassionate to yourself as you'd like other people to be to you.

Write down all your qualities, everything you have to offer, everything on which your true worth is based. Start each sentence with: "I am valuable because …". Remember to add to the list each time you notice something else for which you have value.

This list will no doubt change and develop over time. Tracking what you feel is important enough to list teaches you a great deal about yourself and what you value in yourself. (If you are in any doubt about what you value, turn back to pages 26–29.)

Paradoxically, being able to share generously or give away what you have makes you wealthy. In remote places, people who have little in the material sense share what they have. They show kindness to a stranger; they offer an opportunity to show compassion and kindness

BELOW: Jade can help to create a positive attitude toward money. It assists in clear reasoning and strengthens mental faculties.

in return. Giving our time and our listening skills is just
as valuable as giving a donation, if not more so. A smile
and a word of encouragement cost nothing but could
change a life.

Having the right livelihood has long been one of
the principles of the spiritual path, as has service to
humanity. If you are true to yourself, and you live and
work and have your being in accordance with what you
value, then you are wealthy indeed. Score yourself on
the following wealth points on a scale of 1 to 10.

Wealth Points

SELF-RESPECT A sense of my own worth and value based
on who I am, not what I do.

SELF-ESTEEM A sense of acceptance of myself and my
having achieved a goal no matter how small.

SELF-WORTH A sense of integrity and congruence,
being aligned with my self and honoring my truth.

INNER PEACE (see pages 104–105).

How Well Did You Do? Return to this chapter from time
to time and score yourself as you work through the book.

What Else Enriches My Life?

Spirituality, joy, nature, arts, crafts, music, sports, culture, friendship, hobbies, and community service are all intrinsically rewarding and make life meaningful, giving it passion. Passion is vitality, drive, intention, and sheer joy in living. When you have it, there is no room in your life for doom, gloom, or depression. Passion enables you to find the one thing that you shine at, that makes you unique and special. So, passion is a great life enhancer, as is creativity.

When we create, we put something of our own self into what we produce, whether it is writing, painting, music, or craftwork, and that feels satisfying and good. You'll notice that most of the valuable assets mentioned above do not necessarily entail spending money, although some of them require you to make an effort to do or to be.

BELOW: Polished and naturally smooth stones feel good to the touch and help you to remember your intention.

Friendship

If you have friends with whom you share affection, mutual support, and laughter, who broadly share your world view and your values, and of whose integrity you are in no doubt, then your life is immensely enriched. These are the kind of friends who bring out the best in you, who make you feel richer for knowing them.

34

These are the friends who stimulate inner resources that you didn't know you had: patience, tolerance, and infinite kindness. True friendship is where fun and joy and wonderment lift you up and make you see the world in a different way. But if your so-called friends are needy and constantly drag you down, then perhaps you may need to look at friendship from another angle. Are you with them because they make you feel needed— or superior? Many people confuse being needed and being useful with feeling good about themselves because they believe that, by meeting other people's needs, they must be meeting their own. But is this true? There is a huge difference between supporting a friend when it is appropriate and knowing that, in turn, you receive the same support, making the friendship mutual, to spending endless hours propping up someone who is never there for you. The first one energizes and enriches your life, the second depletes it. Similarly, if you have a friend who constantly tells you how to improve yourself and your life, you are being disempowered by "friendship" rather than empowered. Friends who believe in you and in themselves equally enrich your life. A friend who says "go for it" when you try for a job that seems just out of your league and who helps you practice for the interview is a wonderful gift. As is one who tells you when you are truly out of order and freely forgives you for it. And you, in turn, derive great satisfaction from returning the favor. In other words, friendship is a two-way process, give and take are balanced and the friendship is money in your inner piggy bank. Friendship also makes many of the other inner wealth factors much more fun: sports, art, music, hobbies, and so forth are much more enjoyable when you have a good friend with you.

Spirituality

Many people find great comfort in religion and they may find good companionship through their place of worship, but this is not what spirituality is about. Spirituality means having an inner faith that sustains you and a connection to something greater than you, no matter what name you give to it or, indeed, whether you name it at all. Daily meditation that connects you to this "something greater" and the deep well of peace you experience during meditation immensely enrich your life, and crystals make a perfect focus for meditation.

Service

Being of service is a "state of being" rather than a specific act that you carry out. It comes from being in a place of infinite compassion toward others, from which you do whatever service is needed without thought of reward or recognition. Some of the most potent acts of service are the secret ones that only you know about, performed simply for the joy of giving. A smile is an act of service, as is giving the price of a cup of coffee to a homeless person as long as it's given without judgment or patronage. It is by these small acts that we grow our generosity of spirit and set in motion the flow of prosperity.

Endorphins

BELOW: Ammolite is a gemstone created from the shell of a fossilized sea creature that existed over 65 million years ago.

When you exercise, take a long walk in nature, or eat a piece of chocolate, you are stimulating natural antidepressants within your body, bringing your own feel-good factor into play. When your body is flooded with endorphins it is impossible to feel impoverished, so one of the fastest ways to feel enriched is to exercise.

A small step Ask yourself, "What is the most valuable and enriching thing I could do right now?" Do it!

Clarifying What I Really Want

Knowing what we really want is crucial for prosperity. When we first start to ask the universe for things, or to manifest our inner riches, we tend to be confused about what it is we actually want because we aren't used to focusing on exactly what "it" is. What we think we want can so easily be confused by other, deeper needs. Getting to the bottom of what you really want takes a bit of digging, but is worth it.

Do you really want a big, expensive car that would make you feel good because you'd score a point over all those people who thought you were a loser? Maybe you are trying to bolster your self-image, and it's not about asking for a car at all. In that case, look deeper into what you really want and work on finding that. Perhaps you actually want a serviceable, comfortable car that gets you where you want to go with the minimum of fuss and maximum efficiency. Simply ask for a car. It is questions like this that have to be addressed before you manifest prosperity. Otherwise, not only do mixed messages get sent out but also you are never satisfied when you get what you ask for, because it won't be what you really wanted in the first place.

Ask yourself what you want right at this moment. What would make you feel good? If the answer is a piece of

BELOW: Tiger's Eye and Agate are both grounding and uplifting crystals. They promote personal power, encouraging a positive attitude and confidence in one's own abilities.

chocolate, ask yourself why. Are you seeking the taste and amazing sensation? Do you actually relish each moment it's in your mouth or do you stuff it down so fast you don't taste it? If the taste is what you're after, you're pretty clear on what you want. But if you're stuffing it down, then you're probably just stuffing it down on top of something that threatens to make you feel poor, uncomfortable, somehow lacking or depressed. Maybe it's an endorphin hit you're seeking? Or, perhaps it is a comfort blanket to stop unhappy feelings rising up and taking over. If so, it won't matter how many bars of chocolate you consume, you won't actually feel any better. Sometimes what you really need is a hug or someone to listen and say, "Yes, I know how you feel. It's okay to feel like that."

So, once you've had the "I want" thought, take a moment to clarify exactly what it is you really want. Write down your initial want and keep asking yourself:

* ✳ Is this what I truly want or is it something else?
* ✳ What does this want rest on?
* ✳ What would satisfy my deepest need?
* ✳ What would truly enrich me?

Once you've established what lies beneath what you want, then clearly ask for what you need. Even when you've clarified what you're asking for, other things may get in the way. Ask yourself whether you were ever told: "I want doesn't get," "It's wrong/bad/selfish to want things for yourself," "It's no good wanting," "No good ever comes of wanting things like that."

What else were you told? Take a few moments to contemplate the kind of messages you were given in childhood or have picked up since then. Turn these around into positive statements, such as:

✳ All my needs are met
✳ I have what I want
✳ I wish only good for myself

Giving Yourself What You Want

Go back to a moment in childhood when you really, really, really wanted something. Close your eyes and picture yourself there, feel all the feelings associated with that moment, notice how intense that sense of wanting was.

Did you get it?

How did that make you feel?

If you didn't get what you wanted, change the picture now. Close your eyes again and visualize your younger self being given exactly what you asked for. Feel the excitement, the joy, the satisfaction of being given exactly what you wanted. Remember that you can give yourself that feeling at any moment by giving yourself what you need.

Was it Satisfying?

How long did the satisfaction last? If it was fleeting, it could indicate that there was a deeper need underlying that childish want. Also, note how emotionally attached you were to the outcome. Children are usually strongly attached to outcomes. They think their world will end if they don't get what they want. As an adult, can you feel that intensity of wanting and yet maintain a sense of detachment from the outcome? It is extremely productive when you can be dispassionate about a result.

BELOW: Manifestation Quartz crystals, where one or more crystals can be clearly seen within a larger crystal, are rare. They are invaluable when seeking prosperity.

Ask with clarity Finally, once you know exactly what you want, ask for it clearly and unambiguously in as short a sentence as possible. Practice until you refine your wants into succinct needs.

41

Crystal Prosperity

Wise use of intent involves being in a state of delighted expectancy of manifesting a goal but without emotional investment in the outcome. Paradoxically, although you need to feel an intention with all the positive emotion of which you are capable, you also need to maintain a state of detachment from the outcome that lets it manifest without your will or emotions being involved. We don't need to know why or how intention works because the crystals take care of the process for you, acting as a link to the universal energy manifesting your prosperity.

Intention draws on the power of belief, the written and spoken word, repetition, crystals, the universe, affirmation, and letting go. Ancient peoples understood the power of the spoken and written word and of repetition; that's why they chanted spells and incantations. They wore crystals engraved with protective words or symbols, and gave them to their gods and let them look after the details. It is vital to set an intention and release it out to the world rather than having an expectation of, or emotional investment in, the outcome. Emotional investment is different to emotional involvement. If you are emotionally involved in the initial process, it facilitates manifestation.

BELOW: Prasiolite (Green Amethyst) attracts prosperity through strengthening the mind, emotions, and will.

But emotional investment in the outcome blocks the flow.
You are more likely to be successful if you surrender to
the process once the intention has been put in place.

To Will or Not To Will

To intend or affirm something is to put intention out
to the universe. This does not mean intently focusing
your will and using all your energy to make it happen.
Allowing the process is what it's all about—a dynamic
surrender to something set in motion. It's a bit like
baking a cake. Once you've put all the ingredients
together and placed the cake in the oven, constantly
opening the oven door is counterproductive. All you
get is a flat cake that hasn't cooked properly. But if you
leave the door shut for the requisite time, what you take
out is a beautiful, risen cake.

If you are working with manifestations or
affirmations, putting them in the present tense brings
them into being. If you use the future tense, they are
always in the act of manifesting and don't actually ever
arrive. So say "I do so and so." Saying "I do" brings
your intention into the present moment, whereas
"I will" or "I can" projects it into the future.

43

Trying and Not Trying

Similarly, having an intention is not about trying to do something. As Yoda in *Star Wars* pointed out, you either do or you don't. You can try your whole life long and not get there, but if you do, then you do. It's wise to avoid words such as "no" and "not" and "don't want" when thinking about intention. The subconscious mind doesn't seem to understand how putting "no more" before something, such as "poverty," means that what I really want is "abundance." It just manifests more poverty.

It's also wise not to have an expectation or hidden agenda that "the world owes me." This brings in all kinds of negative feelings and hardly creates the right kind of ambience for your intention to manifest. It's far better to have a goal that moves you positively into the right outcome. So, "I do/I am/I act/I achieve … ".

It's also essential to be careful how you phrase your desire. "Give me more" may bring just that, but it may not be to your benefit or what you expected. If the emotions underlying your intention are unclear, you may well manifest what you craved or feared at your deepest level.

Holding a Clear Intent

Before you frame your intention, read pages 38–41 again. Clarity is essential if you are to manifest prosperity in all its guises.

Affirmations

BELOW: Green Garnet crystals are regenerating stones. They can help you to discard old ways of thinking and patterns that not longer serve a purpose.

Affirmations are statements of what you would like to come about. Phrased positively in the now, they are repeated regularly, preferably while looking into the reflection of your eyes in a mirror. Say your affirmation with all the emotion and intent you can bring to it, and then let go. Well-phrased affirmations do not include "not" or "no" or "anymore." A suitable prosperity affirmation would be: "I am rich in all ways, prosperity flows to me and through me right now."

Take a small step now Start with something small that you believe you can achieve now. Hold the intention, affirm that it is so, let the intention flow into one of your abundance crystals, and then let it go. Surrender to the process.

45

Gratitude and Blessings

Crystal Prosperity

Gratitude is a fundamental part of abundance. Over many religions and thousands of years, people tithed a part of their income or produce to their god. This system worked on a fundamentally sound principle: that of showing gratitude for what the universe had provided or for what you had. It was a way of saying "thank you." You'll be surprised at how showing gratitude for what you have, rather than yearning for what you have not, changes how you feel into a deep sense of enrichment. Counting your blessings is another ancient tradition, one that you can fruitfully use in your own life today.

Some people continue to give a portion of their income to a religious institution or charity. Even if you have no spare money for such projects, you can donate time or used goods, or put your spare produce outside your gate with a notice "please help yourself" to keep the cycle of universal beneficence flowing. Another way of appreciating what you have is to show gratitude and simply say "thank you" even for the smallest things.

BELOW: Keeping a bowl of crystals close to you reminds you to show gratitude in your daily life.

See a Penny

An old man used to say: "See a penny, pick it up, you're
bound to have good luck." He never failed to pick up any
money he saw, no matter how small. And he would always
say "thank you" as he did so. Being an honest soul, if the
money was a large denomination he'd take it to the police
station in case the person who'd lost it enquired. Almost
always, he'd claim it after the requisite time had passed.
As often as not, he'd use it to put a bet on a dog (nowadays
he'd probably buy a lottery ticket). Greyhound racing was
one of his great passions in life. This bet, he said, gave
the money a chance to grow—which it had an uncanny
knack of doing—and, when it did, he shared his good
fortune with family and friends. He was not a wealthy man
in monetary terms, but he was a contented one who was
thankful for his life and for what came his way. He said
that he was blessed: "a joyful witness of life's abundance."

"I Am Blessed"

Counting your blessings helps you to focus on what is
good and positive in your life, turning your attention away
from any perceived lack. Such blessings are not always
the obvious ones.

47

Jade

Citrine

Tiger's Eye

Goldstone

Carnelian

Take time now to write down twenty things in your life for which you feel blessed. These can be anything from the companionship of good friends to an act of kindness from which you have benefited or anything else that comes to your mind.

Once you have got into the habit of thinking of yourself as being blessed, reiterate it often. Affirm "I am blessed" and you are.

Gratitude Rocks

Gratitude rocks help you to be thankful for what you have and to show your appreciation. You can either use an abundance crystal or go out and pick up a rock. Place your gratitude rock where you see it often—by the front door is a good place. Each time you pass it, touch it and say "I am grateful." Each time one of your plans or requests to the universe comes to fruition, add another rock to the pile and say, "thank you." This not only acts as a reminder of how your abundance is stacking up, it reminds you to be thankful, too. You don't have to be thankful to anyone or even for anything; you simply live in a state a gratitude, which some people call grace.

What is the greatest blessing in my life right now?

What is the smallest blessing?

What is my most unexpected blessing?

What is my most exciting blessing?

What has turned out to be a blessing that at first
I thought was a curse?

Do I show my gratitude and appreciation for everything
that is done for me?

Do I show my gratitude and appreciation for what I have?

Am I able to show my gratitude and appreciation for the
things that I don't feel are a blessing but which may be
part of my soul's learning process?

Do I tithe my earnings or my time?

What do I contribute to society?

Chapter 2

Crystal Tools

Crystals are potent tools for prosperity. With their power of attraction and their ability to generate energy, they support and amplify your thoughts, feelings, and emotions and also attract energy toward you. This means that, if you are working with crystals, you need to be sure that those thoughts, feelings, and emotions focus on the positive side of what you want to achieve rather than what you fear might happen. The same applies if you feel sorry for yourself or feel that the world owes you a living. It is much more productive to believe that you support yourself in all ways. Be honest with yourself if you do have fears, because you can also work with crystals to transmute these into positive feelings.

To work at their best, crystals need to be prepared and magnetized. If you ask them specifically to assist in your endeavors, whatever they may be, this avoids any confusion over what a crystal's role in your life is meant to be. The exercises in this chapter can be adapted for other purposes, using the crystals in Chapter 3.

Crystal Prosperity

Intention is your will for something to happen, but it's not a forced will, it's an allowing. In other words, intention is a way of being rather than a way of doing. The best space to be in for the exercises, rituals, and visualizations in this book is one of relaxed but alert attention and focused intent. The clearer your intention is (see pages 42–45), the more quickly what you want to come to pass manifests. And the more you believe your intention manifests, the more you change your world.

Paradoxically, as we have seen, being unattached to the outcome is equally important. Although all your emotions and feelings are focused in the moment you carry out a ritual, layout, or exercise, they are not intent on an outcome. This is a strange idea to grasp, this needing to be passionately involved and yet be unattached to the outcome. It means, however, that if you get out of the way and let things happen, the universe takes over.

Shaped Lavender Jade

Tumbled Amethyst

Amethyst Cluster

Exercise

Aligning With Intent

It is possible to change situations that may appear to be hopeless or intractable using the power of intent alone. To do this, you need to be in a relaxed and attentive state, totally aligned with your highest good. This aligned intentional state is a state in which manifestation takes place, and all possibilities are open at that moment. In a way, it acts outside time and changes situations in a heartbeat. If, for example, you are feeling lonely and alone, you can have the intent that you meet a new friend who enriches your life. Holding the intent is sufficient. You'll be amazed at how quickly the manifestation comes about—particularly if you are being totally unselfish in what you wish for. It is important to stay with being rather than doing— that is, you do not need to do anything, simply to hold the intent, align, and allow. By being in this intentional manifestation space, you do not have to put any further energy into the situation, and it is counterproductive to continually think or emote about it. Let go, let be.

But, you are no doubt wondering, how do you align? Well, practicing with a crystal helps you to recognize how that intentional aligned space feels:

Quartz

Simply hold a Quartz crystal, breathe slowly in and out for five breaths, then ask the crystal to show you how it feels to be fully aligned. Remember that this is a feeling that includes a mental state, so do not expect an intellectual answer. Instead, pay attention to how you feel. You may well experience yourself moving into energetic alignment, with energies moving across and around your spine, and then have a sense of going slightly "up"—indeed, you may lift slightly off your chair or feel the top of your head moving slightly higher. Everyone experiences this alignment in a way that is unique to them, but once you reach it, you know.

Getting the Most from the Exercise:

Sit quietly and ask that your highest energies manifest and that you come into alignment with them. Do not strive to do anything, simply allow and be. Know that by being in this state of quiet intentional alignment, the situation has changed for the better and your intention manifests. Everything has shifted and moved to encompass all possibilities. Bring your attention back into the room, take your attention away and allow the change to manifest.

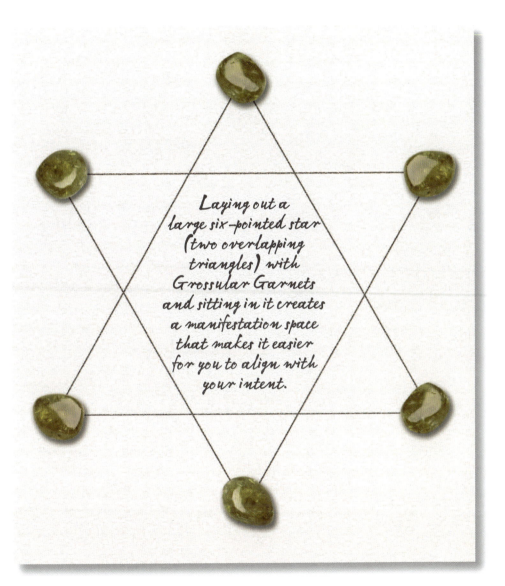

Laying out a large six-pointed star (two overlapping triangles) with Grossular Garnets and sitting in it creates a manifestation space that makes it easier for you to align with your intent.

Crystal Prosperity

Blue Lace Agate

Aventurine

Rose Quartz

Moss Agate

Blue Chalcedony

Crystals *need care. If your crystals are to work at their best, three things need to happen.*

Choose exactly the right crystal for you. As everyone resonates slightly differently, some stones harmonize well with your energies and others do not. (This is why alternative stones are given for specific outcomes.)

Cleanse the crystal of any vibes it has picked up before coming to you and anything it has drawn to itself while in your possession (see page 58). Keep it energetically clean and sparkling in the future.

Magnetize the crystal with focused intent (see below and pages 60–61) so that it attracts to you what you desire. If you don't ask a crystal to work with you, it won't know what to do, and if you don't keep its energies topped off, it goes dead exactly like a battery might. If you are unclear about your intent, then the crystal is also unclear as to exactly what it is you want it to do.

Choosing My Crystals

Your prosperity crystals need to make your heart sing. You can look through the directory at the end of this book and see which crystals call out to you, or do the same in a crystal store. This allows the stones that want to work with you to be attracted toward you. To choose an individual stone out of several possibilities, put your hand into a container of crystals and see which one sticks to your fingers, or touch each one and see which one feels good. If you are in any doubt, hold the crystal over your heart, breathe gently, and see how it feels. If you find you can't put a stone down, this is the crystal for you.

If you're looking for a statement piece, such as an altar stone or a stone for a wealth corner (see pages 92–93), again the feeling of the stone is more important than the look. Sometimes crystals that have been chipped, broken, or scratched actually work harder for you than ones that are perfect. Some crystals have "empathy nicks" that help them to resonate with people's painful feelings and to transmute them.

Choose five crystals from the directory to be your special prosperity stones. Tumbled stones are comfortable to handle and radiate energy equally in all directions, but you may also want to have a crystal point (crystal with a point) that directs energy in a specific way or a geode to hold abundance for you.

Generator Quartz

Cleansing My Crystals

As soon as you get your crystals home or have gathered your crystal collection together, the stones need to be cleansed. Store-bought crystal cleansers are excellent because they transmute any negative energy the crystal has picked up, but you can also use water, salt, or brown rice. Tumbled stones and single-point crystals are easily cleansed under running water or in salt water. Crystal clusters or fragile stones need care because water can easily penetrate the cracks and loosen individual points or layers. These are best placed in brown rice overnight. Regularly cleanse all your stones.

ABOVE: Placing non-friable crystals in a bowl of salt clears negative energy.

Energizing My Crystals

Some of the store-bought crystal cleansers reenergize the stones, but all crystals benefit from being out in sunlight for a few hours, and white stones enjoy moonlight.

Magnetizing My Crystals

Once your crystal has been cleansed and energized, it needs to be dedicated to working for your highest good. Hold the crystal in your hands for a few moments to attune to it, then ask it to work with you always for your highest good and to help you enjoy an abundant life. If you have a specific task for the crystal to assist with, state it clearly and precisely (see pages 60–61).

Storing My Crystals

Crystals prefer to be out there working rather than being shut away, but sometimes even the most willing crystal needs a rest or your priorities change. Always cleanse a crystal before putting it away. If you no longer need it to perform a specific task, tell the crystal so. Thank it for its work on your behalf, and ask it to continue to support your well-being. While crystals that are not working enjoy sunlight, this can fade the color, so do not leave them on windowsills or in direct sunlight. Similarly, crystals can be damaged by being left outdoors, so do check yours regularly if outside. (If you are leaving crystals outdoors, rough pieces are less susceptible to damage.) Your bigger crystals enjoy being displayed on shelves, for you to luxuriate in their beauty, and smaller crystals can be wrapped or placed in a mandala or other pleasing layout.

Keep your five prosperity crystals together in a pouch when not in use, carefully wrapping any points, and place them in the wealth corner of a room (see pages 92–93).

Crystal energy is powerful, but so too is the extraordinary ability of your mind to create, especially when this is amplified by the energies of crystals. The power of your mind works through language, images, and beliefs, which interact with symbols and crystals to co-create your world. But crystals also work with your emotions, and harnessing emotions to your intention amps up the energy even further. Indeed, without strongly feeling your intention, little is likely to change. When seeking prosperity, you need to feel it, taste it, smell it. In other words, put your whole being into manifesting it through the crystal and then leave the crystal to do its work.

Clarifying Intent

Crystals pick up anything and everything you are thinking and feeling—which is why the first chapter of this book concentrated on establishing exactly how you viewed prosperity and just what you were seeking before you started to work with your crystals.

So, before you magnetize a crystal for any of the rituals or layouts that follow, take a few moments to clarify your intent and to ensure that you are holding a positive focus for the outcome. If you have any doubts or fears, work through these, if necessary with the assistance of a crystal, before you charge up your crystal with intent.

Putting Intention Into a Crystal

When you know exactly what your intent is, hold the thought in your mind and feel all the positive emotions associated with manifesting it: joy, fulfillment, excitement, purpose, and so on. Then hold the crystal in your hands, speak your intent out loud, and pour your intention and all those good feelings into the crystal as you do so. Ask the crystal that it takes this intention out to the world and manifests it. This magnetizes the crystal. Then withdraw your attention. Place the crystal in an appropriate place, and simply trust that your intention comes into being in the right way and with the right timing.

Fluorite

Always remember to cleanse and magnetize your crystals before using them for rituals or layouts.

The Prosperity Ritual

Deep introspection into what you truly believe is an essential part of the prosperity ritual—an examination that takes at least three days. The dark period between the death of the old moon and the rise of the new is a perfect time to do it, because it assists you in going inward to explore your deepest beliefs. Once you have focused your mind and feelings on what prosperity really means for you, you are ready to carry out this ritual.

TOOLS White or silver notebook and pen; mineral salts or Halite crystal; white flowers; candles and holders; cloth; crystals such as Quartz, Clear Elestial Quartz, Moonstone, White Calcite, White Jade.

RIGHT: Take time to prepare the area where you are going to carry out the ritual. White flowers stand out in a low-lit space and during a candlelit ritual.

62

TIMING Use the three dark days of the old moon to examine your beliefs about prosperity. Perform the ritual at new moonrise to sow the seeds of your prosperity, or at full moon to bring a project to fruition.

PREPARATION Read your answers to the questions posed in Chapter 1. From these responses and any additional insights, consider exactly what prosperity means to you. Initially, write your thoughts as a "stream of consciousness" in which everything you personally believe and think about prosperity pours onto the page. Don't censor and don't judge what you write, simply allow it to be.

When you're sure you've emptied all your thoughts and beliefs about prosperity into the notebook, read through what you've written from a standpoint of compassionate witnessing— that is, don't judge yourself for having these thoughts and beliefs. Recognize that they are simply that—thoughts and beliefs. You are more than the programs your mind is running. Be gentle with yourself.

RIGHT: Use a notebook to jot down your thoughts as they occur to you, no matter how randomly.

Distill the major points and write them in your notebook in the form of statements, such as:

I believe that prosperity is …
To me, prosperity means …
To be prosperous, I have to: …
I do not feel prosperous because …
I am already prosperous because …
I feel that other people are prosperous because …

Add any other headings that are appropriate.

Now breathe into your heart, focus all your attention there, and allow your heart to expand. Feel yourself connecting to your deep inner self that is beyond your ego or your personality. From a place of the love within your heart and your true self for the you that is having all these struggles and beliefs, go through the list and ask yourself how much you truly believe in these things. You can also ask yourself from where these thoughts and beliefs about prosperity stem. You'll no doubt find that many of them have been inculcated into your mind by your parents and the people who were around you when you were a child or a young adult. If you no longer accept them as true, ask yourself what is true for you now in this present moment, and write those answers in your notebook. Sleep on your answers overnight, and then read them through again. Ask yourself once more: "Is this really true for me now?" If it is, write it on a new page. If it's not, write down what is true for you at this moment in time. Distill the essence of these statements into a sentence that begins:

> *For me, true prosperity is ...*
> Make a note of this on a piece of paper so that you read it aloud as part of the ritual.

PLACE If the weather is suitable, this ritual is particularly potent carried out somewhere in nature where your crystals are under the direct light of the full or the rising new moon. If not, then choose a windowsill—if possible, one that faces the rising moon—on which to place your crystals.

The Ritual

✳ Prepare yourself carefully. If the weather is warm and there is a suitable place, you could bathe yourself and your crystals in the sea, a lake, or a river. If not, have a bath with a handful of mineral salts, or hang a small bag of salt or Halite under the showerhead to wash over you as you shower.

✳ Dedicate your crystals and charge them with the intention of attracting to yourself and discovering within you true prosperity.

✳ Place your candles around you and, as you light each one, say aloud: "I ignite the flame of true prosperity within myself and invite it to manifest in the world."

✳ Take the piece of paper on which you have written what true prosperity means to you and read it out loud. Then place it in a central place.

✳ Take your white flowers and place them around the paper, saying out loud: "I invite the powers of nature to unite with me in true prosperity."

White Chalcedony

Snow Quartz

✳ Finally, surround your piece of paper with white crystals and, if you have a large crystal, place this in the center. As you blow out the candles, state out loud that you invite prosperity into your life right now.

✳ Leave the crystals in place for two weeks. If the flowers wither, compost them saying, "Let these flowers make fertile compost for my prosperity."

✳ Each time you notice how much more prosperous you feel in any way, make a note of it in your notebook, thanking the crystals for their work in drawing this to you.

✳ After two weeks, thank the crystals for their work and dismantle the circle. Take the crystals out and "plant" them somewhere in nature. Place the paper in your notebook.

✳ Allow your prosperity to grow without investing emotional energy into the outcome.

Quartz

Moonstone

67

The Inner-Wealth Ritual

Topaz

Jade

Malachite

True wealth has nothing to do with how much money we have. It is the qualities within us and those we share with the world around us—our hidden resources—that make us truly wealthy. But! Our inner riches are often so well hidden that we perceive them only in other people, or we do not give value to what we have until we think deeply and recognize that good friends, for instance, are part of our wealth. This ritual helps you to find these inner riches for yourself.

TOOLS Notebook and pen; Jade, Topaz, or other introspective prosperity crystal; candle and holder.

TIMING The dark of the moon—the three days just before new moon.

PREPARATION Set aside time when you can be peacefully introspective with no interruptions. You can either do the preparatory work for this ritual in two parts on separate days, allowing time for new insights to arise, or you can do it the day before new moon, doing the first part in the morning, the second in the afternoon, and the third in the evening. This allows time for new insights to arise, but you can also add insights that arise after the ritual if you leave space in your notebook, and claim these qualities as your own.

68

What Do I See In You?

Turn back to the list you made of ten people you admire (see page 27) and write this in your notebook, spacing the names out well.

- What were the particular qualities that made these people special to you? Note them against each name.
- What do these people specifically contribute to your life? Make a note.

We frequently admire in other people qualities that we seek but do not recognize in ourselves. So:

- Is there a specific quality or qualities that come up repeatedly? If so, note it or them below the list under the heading "Qualities I would like to own in myself."

We often contribute more than we realize to the lives of other people. So:

- If the people on your list are personally known to you, ask them to list what you contribute to their lives.
- Do you recognize these qualities in yourself?

And finally:

- Write down your twenty best qualities.
- Ask a friend to write down your twenty best qualities.

How do the lists compare?

Ask yourself: "Do I believe I have these qualities?"

69

Crystal Prosperity

Have I tapped into my inner worth?

Do I truly value me?

Do I have good friends?

Is there a way to increase my friendship quotient?

How mutual are my friendships?

Does everything go one way in my friendships?

Is this flow to me or away from me? (If it's to you, you may need to change your friendship habits.)

Do I need to shed some of my old needy friends and find new ones?

What kind of friend would make me feel fulfilled?

Do I make time in my life for enriching activities?

If not, can I program some time in?

Do I meditate or have another spiritual practice?

How do I serve others?

Could I volunteer in any capacity?

What activities could I engage in that would enrich my life?

Do I engage in creative activities?

Did I engage in creative activities as a child or young adult?

If there are things I'd like to do but don't, what's stopping me?

Is there something new to try?

The Ritual

✳ If you find background music relaxing, play something slow and introspective that helps you to move deeper into yourself. Dim the lights.

✳ Settle yourself comfortably somewhere you will not be disturbed and light your candle. Place it in front of you. Read through your notebook and, on a separate piece of paper, make a list of all the qualities that you admire or that you see within yourself and others.

✳ Pick up your piece of Jade, breathe gently, and relax. Spend a few moments looking at your piece of Jade. Feel its quiet confidence, its strength, and its serenity. Let these qualities travel through your hands, up your arms, and into your heart.

✳ When you are ready, pick up your list of qualities in your other hand and look at the first one. Can you own it within yourself? If yes, touch the Jade to your heart, say out loud: "I own and honor my ...." Check off the quality on your list and move on to the next one.

✳ If no, then quietly affirm to yourself: "I am/have ...," "I own my ...," "my ... is part of my inner wealth," "I honor my ...," "I am grateful for my ...," "and I am ready to show my ... to the world." When you believe it, touch your Jade to your heart, check off the quality on your list, and move on. So, for example: I have integrity, I own my integrity, my

Jade

72

integrity is part of my inner wealth, I honor my integrity, I am grateful for my integrity, and I am ready to show my integrity to the world.

✳ Repeat this affirmation for every quality on your list.

If you find it difficult to own qualities, simply sit quietly repeating to yourself "I am …," until you believe it.

So, for example, "I am integrity, I am integrity, I am integrity, I am integrity."

✳ Repeat the whole affirmation out loud, touch the Jade to your heart, and put a check mark by the quality on your list.

✳ When you have completed the whole list, spend a few moments contemplating this reservoir of inner wealth.

All these enriching qualities within you; this heartfelt store of riches.

✳ When you are ready to end the ritual, blow out the candle, saying: "I send my riches out to the world in blessing and in gratitude."

✳ Place the list where you see it often and place the Jade under your pillow.

✳ Enjoy your inner wealth and let it shine out to the world.

✳ Repeat the ritual weekly until you have discovered all your hidden qualities, and have put them into practice in your world.

The Abundance Layout

Crystal Prosperity

Abundance is about living fully, physically, mentally, emotionally, and spiritually. Generating and drawing abundance to you entails mental and emotional focus, opening your mind to the new possibilities that living in the abundant universe opens up for you. This ritual connects you to the spiritual abundance all around and helps you to live abundantly. It builds on the work you have already done to recognize what true abundance is and how it enriches your life (see Chapter 1).

TOOLS Five cleansed and magnetized prosperity stones (Tiger's Eye, Carnelian, Citrine, Jade, Goldstone, or other stones of your choice), brightly colored cloth, your abundance treasure map (see pages 96–97) or the template on page 75, 3 feet (1 meter) of cord.

TIMING This layout is particularly effective at full moon.

PREPARATION Read through your answers to the questions in Chapter 1. Prepare an abundance treasure map (see page 96), including all the things that you have identified as making you feel abundant, not just those related to material wealth. Lay out your cloth and place your abundance treasure map or the template in the center when you are ready to begin. Hold the intention that this layout helps you to manifest true abundance in your life.

The Spiral of Abundance

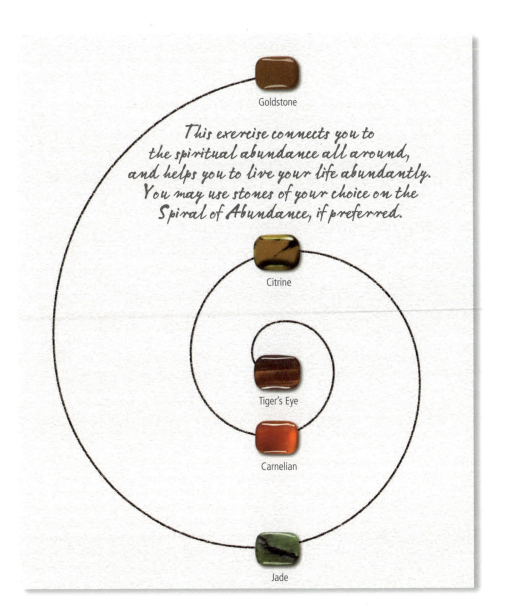

Goldstone

This exercise connects you to
the spiritual abundance all around,
and helps you to live your life abundantly.
You may use stones of your choice on the
Spiral of Abundance, if preferred.

Citrine

Tiger's Eye

Carnelian

Jade

The Layout

✳ Choose a place for this layout where you can leave the treasure map undisturbed. The wealth corner of your house (see pages 92–93) is ideal for this layout.

✳ Place your treasure map or template on a brightly colored cloth. Starting at the center of your treasure map, lay a cord spiral out to the edge. If you don't have time to make a treasure map, you can simply use the template on page 75 as an alternative.

✳ Sit quietly holding your prosperity stones in your hands and reflect on what you have already learned about abundance and true prosperity. Allow yourself to expand and open up to the abundant universe that wishes only the best for you, linking yourself to it through the crystals in your hands. Smile and open your heart to receive that abundance—hold your crystals to your heart as you do so.

✳ Now take that smile down into the creative center at the base of your belly, allowing your hand and your crystals to rest in your lap.

✳ Keeping hold of your stones in one hand, use the other to place the stones.

✳ Lay your Tiger's Eye stone at the center of the spiral. As you lay it, focus your attention on the abundance that surrounds you right now, your base security. Feel how grounded and supported you are by the earth beneath your feet, how rich you already are at your root. If you become aware of any financial worries intruding, let the stone reassure you; allow yourself to feel its strength and security, surrender the worries to the stone, and bathe in its abundant energy.

✳ Now take the hand holding the crystals up to just below your navel. Pick out the Carnelian and hold it in your other hand for a moment. Feel its bright energy radiating out and allow yourself to absorb that energy. This activates your abundance attractor factor. Place the stone on the cord spiral and focus your attention on attracting even more abundance in your life; how you open to receive this beautiful gift of the universe.

✳ Now take your hand and the crystals up to your solar plexus. Hold the Citrine in your other hand, and feel the generosity of its energy radiating out from the stone. Feel the bubbles of joy it imparts to your solar plexus. Place the Citrine on the spiral and feel the emotional abundance in your life, the good friends, the family, the warm feelings that support you, and your own emotional generosity. Give thanks for those friends and that emotional abundance, and for the generosity of spirit that you share.

✳ Now take your crystals up to your heart and hold your Jade in your other hand. As you place the Jade on the spiral, let it absorb and transform any fear or self-pity of which you may have become aware and allow it to assist you to receive with grace and thankfulness. Then ask the stone to help you to find the richness in your heart and open that out to draw abundance to you at every level.

✳ Finally, take your hand with the Goldstone up above your head. Feel the transmutative energy of the Goldstone radiating down through the core of your being, connecting you to the spiritual abundance that floods through every level of your life. As you place the stone at the end of the spiral, let that spiritual abundance flow out into the world and into the future. See its sparkling particles imbuing that future with even more abundance, simply waiting

Tiger's Eye

Carnelian

for you to reach it and effortlessly harvest it and incorporate it into your life. Now bring your attention to the treasure map that is underpinning your spiral. Picture the spiral turning and bringing all those abundant things into your life right now, manifesting more and more of your abundance into your present reality. Feel how this abundance enriches your life. Enjoy!

✳ Gazing at your spiral, recognize how from being grounded in the creative root of your being, you expand and flow outward and upward, becoming more and more abundant in your life and sharing that abundance generously with your world.

✳ Thank the crystals for helping you and, if possible, leave the spiral in place to do its work. If this is not possible, leave the stones where you can see them.

BELOW: The abundance crystals shown are all powerful and dynamic. They all teach how to manifest and attract wealth, prosperity, success, and positivity.

Citrine

Jade

Goldstone

Potency and belief generate cash. How easily you are able to generate money depends on several things, and one of the major causes of not generating money is the beliefs you have about yourself. So, the first part of the work involves changing any toxic thoughts about money you might have. It also helps to believe that money flows to you through the blessing of the universe; you don't have to work for every penny. The second part involves laying a grid in your home or your place of work. Choose places for the crystals where they will not be disturbed, and remember to cleanse them regularly.

TOOLS Aventurine, Turquoise, or other appropriate stone (raw chunks or tumbled stones can be used); lottery ticket (optional). Because the grid follows the Chinese feng shui grid, you could choose stones that correspond to each area of life (see pages 92–93).

TIMING If using Turquoise for this grid, lay it out at new moon. If using other stones, lay it out between the new and full moon.

PREPARATION Take time to review the money script that runs in your head without you really being conscious of it: the kind of things that you were told in childhood or which you have absorbed from your culture, the negative

Turquoise

expectations you have. Before you go any further, ask yourself if you've ever said or been told:

- You have to work incredibly hard to have money.
- There'll never be enough.
- People like us don't do things like that.
- Money is the root of all evil.
- The world owes me a living.
- I'll never get out of debt.
- I don't deserve that.
- You're not good enough.
- There's virtue in poverty.
- I'm not clever enough/good enough.
- That's my dream but it won't generate money, so I can't do it.
- You can't turn your passion into a career.
- Be realistic.
- I don't have the right accent and clothes to do that kind of a job.
- I didn't go to the right kind of school, so I'll never have/get a good job.
- I can only be happy if I have money.

If needed, use the exercise that follows to alter your mental blueprint before you lay out the generating money grid.

81

Exercise

Crystal Prosperity

Changing Your Mental Blueprint

✳ Revisit pages 22–25 and pages 68–73 and take another look at some of the fixed points on your mental blueprint, those toxic thoughts imprinted in childhood and by your cultural core beliefs. To release these, hold a prosperity stone in your hand, close your eyes, and think about each negative belief.

✳ As you do so, deliberately choose the opposite belief. Say out loud the positive belief and lay down the crystal on the mandala opposite to affirm the positive belief that replaces the negative. Repeat this process for each negative belief so that you build up a new mental blueprint for yourself, one that is abundant and prosperous and that leaves room for all the other things that enrich your life.

✳ Now open your eyes and look at how many positive beliefs enrich your life. You may like to make a mandala with the stones in the success part of your house (see pages 92–93) and then leave them in place to remind you of how rich your life is.

✳ This mandala makes a perfect focus for daily meditation; gaze at it, letting your eyes go out of focus and quietening your breathing while you observe the stones. Do not try to make anything happen, simply allow. Notice how different you feel after a week of doing this.

Tiger's Eye

This mandala can be used as a blank template on which you can place up to twenty-one prosperity stones.

The Grid

You could choose the wealth corner (see pages 92–93) for this, or place the stones on the larger template on page 154 of this book. Orientate the grid so that the top left-hand corner is facing the same direction as the wealth corner of your house—that is, the far left-hand corner at the back. Alternatively, use your whole home as a grid, and place the stones accordingly. If you have a lottery ticket, place it in the center of the grid.

✴ Focus your intention and lay your first stone on point A on the grid, saying out loud: *"I am generating money, I set this generation in motion now."*

✴ Lay your second stone on point B, saying:
"Money grows ever larger."

✴ Lay your third stone on point C and say:
"Money grows without boundaries."

✴ Lay your fourth stone on point D and say:
"Money arrives from unexpected sources."

✴ Lay your fifth stone on point E and say:
"Money flows freely."

✴ Lay your sixth stone on point F and say:
"Money increases moment by moment."

✳ Lay your seventh stone on point G and say:

"Money grows and grows."

✳ Lay your eighth stone on point H and say:

"Money flows freely to me from all directions in all ways."

✳ Look at the center of the grid and picture a pile of money growing until it spills abundantly all over the grid. Feel that money growing and your sense of joyful abundance increasing.

✳ Say *"thank you"* for the abundance that flows to you.

✳ Withdraw your attention and your emotion.

✳ Leave the grid to do its work.

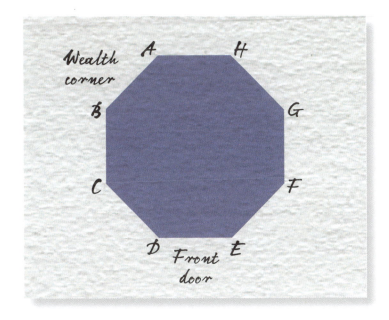

RIGHT: The Generating Money grid is provided in larger scale on page 154. Focus your attention on the stones as you repeat each affirmation.

Finding the Perfect Job Ritual

Perfect jobs *are out there for everyone. This ritual draws on the previous work you have done and requires you to focus even more deeply into what it is that you really want. It is equally suitable for finding your dream career as it is for finding a fill-in job while at college. Both should be as fulfilling as possible and bring you what you need.*

TOOLS Small gold notebook and pen; golden cloth; six tumbled Golden Tiger's Eyes; gold candle in a suitable holder and matches.

NOTE YOU CAN USE RED TIGER'S EYE TUMBLED STONES IF YOU FEEL MORE ATTRACTED TO THIS COLOR, IN WHICH CASE CHOOSE A DARK RED OR PINK NOTEBOOK, CLOTH, AND CANDLE FOR THE RITUAL.

TIMING This ritual is particularly effective at new moon, but it works whenever you feel ready to do it. You can prepare in the days leading up the new moon, doing a question before you go to bed, or you could do the whole thing in a day. Sleep on the answers for at least one night to allow fresh insights to arise before you complete the ritual.

PREPARATION Take your phone off the hook and put a "Do not disturb" notice on your door. Ensure that you have sufficient time, whether you are completing the

Tumbled Tiger's Eye

86

preparation and ritual in one session or in several smaller sections.

- If you find music soothing, play suitable background music, or prepare in silence.
- Sit quietly and focus your thoughts inward. Let the distractions of the outer world slip away.
- Remind yourself that your intent is to find a new and fulfilling job, and that the ritual is to bring that job into manifestation.
- Breathe gently, focusing on your breath. As you breathe out, allow any tension you may be feeling to drop away. As you breathe in, feel yourself filling up with a sense of peace and relaxation.
- When you feel ready, pick up your pen and notebook and ask yourself what you most want out of a job. Be specific and precise, but don't censor what comes into your mind. Be open to all possibilities and paradoxes—you can always train or retrain for a different career.
- If you have a particular salary in mind, say so but don't limit it; saying "above $ … per year" opens the possibility of a higher salary than you envisage.
- If you want to work in a specific location, pinpoint it—or open it up to wherever is appropriate for you.

Red Tiger's Eye

87

- If you need a particular level of responsibility, specify it. If job satisfaction matters most to you, say so, and so on.
- But remember, if what you are looking for is simply a fill-in job, something to generate money for the time being, or to serve as a step in the right direction rather than being your ultimate goal, this is acceptable, too. Simply be honest with yourself about what you want, and include the time frame "for the time being" or, if possible, give yourself a time frame that says "… and by [specify date] I move on from this job to something even better."
- Leaving the first page blank, write each point in your notebook.

Give it plenty of space.
Let it breathe.

- Then list all the skills and experience you bring to this new job.
- Now think about your goals and write those in the notebook. Be specific about your timing, objectives, and anticipated outcome. Remember to add "this or something better."

- Contemplate alternatives and think laterally. Is there a different area in which you could use your skills? Could you retrain? Is there something you've always wanted to do but never had the opportunity? List it all!

- Now check out any inherent contradictions in what you have written. Ask yourself if the desired outcome is in accord with your highest ideals and your deepest integrity. If there is a contradiction, how do you feel about it? Does expediency trump ideology? Can you encompass the contradictions for the time being? Or are there areas where you just cannot go? If there are, list them. Be absolutely clear about what is acceptable to you and what is not.

- When you have finished writing, place the notebook under your pillow. Tell yourself that if any further insights that you need rise up into your consciousness during the night, try to remember them so that you can note them down when you wake. Pay particular attention to any dreams that you may have and make a note of these, whether or not they seem relevant at the time.

The Ritual

✳ Have a bath or shower and put on clean clothes. Dim the lights. If you like, play suitable background music, or work the ritual in silence.

✳ Now calmly retrieve your notebook and carefully read through it.

✳ Distill the essence of what you want from this new job into one sentence and write it in the front of your notebook, starting, "My new job is ...." (You may also want to make a note of this on a piece of paper to read aloud as part of the ritual.)

✳ Spread the cloth onto a table and place the candle on the notebook in the center. Then place the six Tiger's Eyes around the candle slowly and deliberately in a Star of David pattern: two overlapping triangles with one point up to release your intention out to the universe, and the second point down to draw it into manifestation. As you place the stones, say: "I place these stones to bring my new job into manifestation."

✳ Light the candle and look deep into the flame.

✳ Affirm to yourself that the job is already there for you, waiting to come into manifestation right now.

Tiger's Eye

✳ Call your new job into being. Putting as much feeling and intention as possible into your words, read out the sentence that sums up the essence of your new job, starting, "My new job is ..." and ending, "and I call it into being now."

✳ Put your hand on your heart and picture being in this job, how you feel, the satisfaction and excitement it gives you. See yourself doing the job as the future stretches out before you and pull that future into the ever-present now. Put as much emotion as possible into the seeing.

✳ When you are ready, blow out the candle, sending your intention for this job into the universe with the smoke. Thank the universe for granting your request. Be confident that it returns to you in tangible form. Let it go.

✳ Leave the notebook in the center of the stones for several days. Each morning light the candle and call your new job into being, feeling delighted anticipation as you do so. Thank the universe for listening. Then blow out the candle and trust that it manifests in the best way possible for you.

✳ Each time you blow the candle out, remove your focus and your emotion from the Star of David, but be ready to spot any opportunity that comes your way.

Star of David

The Wealth Corner

Crystal Prosperity

Wealth corners are found in Chinese feng shui, an ancient method of bringing energetic harmony into your home. There are various systems, some of which are based on the compass, but the easiest way to divide your house up is from the front door. This puts the wealth corner at the far back left-hand corner of the house or a room.

In feng shui, parts of the home relate to your business success (the area around your front door) and your fame or personal success (the area on the opposite side of the house to the front door). As you go in the front door, scholarly success is found on the left-hand side of the business area, with a good family life between it and the wealth corner. The area of success for your children is on the right-hand side, between the relationship corner on the far right and international trade and/or mentors is in the right-hand corner beside your front door (see illustration). To attract or enhance success in any of these areas, place suitably magnetized large crystals in the appropriate area.

(Front) Door

International Trade / Mentors	Business Success	Scholarly Success
Children's Success		Family
Relationships	Fame/Personal Success	Wealth

Generator Quartz

The Wealth Corner

Citrine is ideal for the wealth corner. If your wealth corner is situated in an area where money flows in and straight out again—as if a bathroom is placed here—a Citrine geode helps you to preserve your money. As long as there is no sink spot for the money to flow down, placing a generator-shape stone or cluster generates wealth for your home.

The Feng Shui Prosperity Stone

Iridescent Ammolite flashes six-colored fire and has been dubbed the feng shui prosperity stone. It creates, conserves, and emanates prosperity on all levels. Each color represents a specific type of prosperity. Choose crystals of specific colors to stimulate appropriate areas.

Ammolite

Red: Energy and growth

Orange: Increased sexual energy and creativity

Green: Entrepreneurship and wisdom

Yellow: Wealth and intellectual prosperity

Blue: Peace and good health

Purple: Spiritual well-being and evolution.

Blessings were sought in ancient times when people petitioned the gods for good fortune for a new venture. Their chosen tool was a crystal—stones still exist with such petitions engraved on them. Nowadays, you can request a blessing from whichever divine being resonates with you or from the universe.

White Calcite

Moonstone

Iron Pyrite

Crystal shapes are particularly useful for inaugurating new ventures. An egg shape is like a seed: it hatches into something bigger when the time is right. A sphere represents fullness: it has no limitations, all possibilities are open and can be realized. A point draws the energy in or sends it out to the universe, depending on which way it is pointing.

TOOLS Iron Pyrite, Moonstone, White Calcite, or other stones representing new beginnings. An egg- or sphere-shape crystal is ideal.

THE ANGELS *New beginnings:* Ariel, Gazardiel. *Success:* Perpetiel, Barakiel, Anauel. *Abundance:* Barbelo.

TIMING New ventures are best started on a new moon or in the period leading up to full moon. Avoid starting a new venture on a waning moon or during the dark of the moon. Astrologically speaking, new ventures are auspicious when started at the commencement of a new Jupiter cycle, which takes place every twelve years from your birth.

PREPARATION Before you ask for the blessing, take time for introspection. Ensure that your venture accords with your ideals and your deepest integrity. Set out your intentions for the venture clearly. Your venture does not have to be something that earns money, but if it is and you need to earn a specific amount, specify this and add "or something greater." If you are intending to help people, make that a goal. Cleanse your crystal and magnetize it for success before commencing the blessing.

THE BLESSING Holding your crystal in your hands, call down the blessing of your chosen angel, divinity, or the universe on your venture and into the crystal. So, for example, you could use the following words:

> "I ask the great Archangel Ariel to pour blessings on my new venture for the highest good of all concerned, bringing it success and abundance now and always, and I ask that this crystal attunes to your blessing and radiates it out for the benefit of all. Thank you, Ariel, for your assistance in this venture."

Place your crystal in an appropriate place, such as the relevant success section of your home or place of work.

Treasure Maps

Crystal Prosperity

Treasure maps are fun to make and should be made with focused intention. Treasure maps help you to focus on exactly what you would like to manifest and to be specific in your choices. To make one, first collect together pictures or phrases that illustrate exactly what you want. Look through old magazines or brochures and keep an eye out for anything appropriate. If you're looking for your ideal house, for instance, collect pictures of houses that appeal to you, floor plans that work for you, and interior design ideas you'd like to incorporate.

TOOLS Large piece of thin cardboard and clip frame; pictures or photographs; small crystals; glue stick.

TIMING You can make a treasure map at any time.

Treasure Map

Lay out your pictures to the same size as your piece of cardboard so that you have an attractive arrangement. If appropriate, place a photo of yourself in the center (choose a happy, smiling one).

Carefully glue the pictures and phrases onto your cardboard. As you place them, say to yourself: *"I am creating exactly what I want, I call this into being now."*

96

Insert into a clip frame, then decorate the frame by gluing small pieces of crystal around the edge, or place the cardboard into a frame onto which you have glued crystals. Display it where you see it often. Remember not to make an emotional investment into the outcome; you succeed far more quickly if you remain detached.

Chapter 3

Crystals for Specific Outcomes

Crystal tools to assist in manifesting or supporting your prosperity in specific areas of your life can be found in this chapter. These can be combined with the rituals and layouts in Chapter 2 to cover all your prosperity needs. Simply use your imagination and a little ingenuity to match the techniques and crystals for specific outcomes. A variety of crystals are given, so choose the one that speaks to you or one to which you have already been attracted and, therefore, have in your collection. Always remember to cleanse and magnetize crystals before use. Having magnetized a crystal, you can wear it, carry it with you, or place it in the wealth corner of your home (see pages 92–93).

Crystal healers use the chakra system of the body and corresponding color to support their healing work, and you can use these subtle energy centers to support your prosperity. Certain issues, such as poverty consciousness or a lack of basic security, pertain to particular chakras. By placing crystals on the appropriate chakras (see page 155), you transmute the negative issue into positive prosperity consciousness. Stones have also long been linked to the organs of the body and are placed over those organs to transmute the negative feelings associated with them: fear with the kidneys, anger with the liver, grief with the lungs, and so on.

Managing your money means more than having a budget and sticking to it. There are always unexpected demands on your purse, but if you are in an ever-flowing energy stream, the money and the resources you need are irresistibly attracted toward you and there is always enough to go around.

Sensible Spending

Wearing Green Quartz helps you to stop hemorrhaging money and to make sensible budgetary choices. It also assists you in being charitable to yourself and to others. Jet and Peridot are ancient aids for stabilizing the finances.

Jet

Planning a Budget

Green Spinel helps in budgeting and sorting out a financial mess, as does Cinnabar or Peridot. Hold the crystal for a few moments and allow creative solutions to rise up into your mind. Wear a bracelet of magnetized prosperity stones to remind you of your budget when in areas of temptation, such as stores and when browsing the Internet.

Becoming More Creative With Money

Finding new ways to grow your money without risks is a process assisted by Goldstone or Malachite. Hold the

Peridot

Goldstone

Malachite

crystal in your hands and ask that the way be opened to creative use of your money. Watch for opportunities that come your way. Peridot is a crystal of financial and spiritual abundance. It assists you in leaving behind old habits, such as spending too much or being miserly, and shows how to be creative with what you have. This stone puts out to the universe that you are ready to accept abundance right now.

CHAKRA SUPPORT SYSTEM Poverty consciousness is an issue connected to the base chakra. To reverse a sense of lack or a blocked energy flow, place brown crystals over the earth chakra beneath your feet, red crystals over your base chakra (see page 155), orange ones over your sacral chakra, and green or pink stones over your heart. To stimulate the earth chakra and ground yourself in the material world, place brown crystals and earthy grounding stones, such as Hematite, on your feet.

SUGGESTED EXERCISES Prosperity ritual (pages 62–67), inner-wealth ritual (pages 68–73), abundance layout (pages 74–79), generating money grid (pages 80–85), wealth corner (pages 92–93).

101

Crystal Prosperity

Prosperity is not purely a matter of having money, but there are times when you need cash in a hurry. Stones in this chapter also attract other resources you may need.

Peridot

Attracting Money

Put a Citrine, Jet, or Yellow Sapphire in your purse or money box, and Carnelian at the entrance to your home to attract money. Green Grossular Garnet manifests the money you want for necessities or fun. Place Garnets in a Star-of-David pattern (one triangle over another) around a piece of paper on which you have written the amount of money you need and what you specifically require it for. If possible, place it under the new moon. Peridot attracts money you need; keep one in your purse or on bills awaiting payment to create a healthy flow.

If money is slow to arrive, visualize a large spiral of Green Spinels spinning rapidly over your bed to bring you a legacy or other money that is slow in coming. Picture another spiral over the mailbox to draw in wins on a lottery or other randomly generated opportunity.

Green Grossular Garnet

To Use Money Wisely

Green Tourmaline helps you to appreciate what you have and to allocate your money in the wisest way so that you always have enough. It assists you in being creative in how you manage your money, opening your eyes to new possibilities, such as recycling what you have, bartering, or other energy exchange, or spotting a volunteering or other opportunity that keeps the energy flowing. Prehnite supports your ability to take sensible risks and encourages your own "inner knowing" to prompt you when a not-to-be-missed opportunity comes along.

Prehnite

Carnelian

CHAKRA SUPPORT SYSTEM   Creation and attraction is an issue connected with the sacral chakra. Orange stones placed on this area assist you in drawing in all the money and other resources that you need.

SUGGESTED EXERCISES   Prosperity ritual (pages 62–67), inner-wealth ritual (pages 68–73), abundance layout (pages 74–79), generating money grid (pages 80–85), wealth corner (pages 92–93).

Inner Peace

Peace is a wealth that no one can take away from you, and only you can find it in the stillness of your inner being. With inner peace safely anchored in your heart, nothing knocks you off balance or makes you doubt yourself. Richness indeed. Spending fifteen minutes with your crystals night and morning helps you to still your mind and reach this peace deep within yourself. Wearing one constantly reminds you of your unshakable core of inner peace.

To Find Inner Serenity

Jade is a serenity stone that is highly prized for its connection to wisdom garnered in tranquillity. Contemplate it several times a day to connect to inner peace. Wearing Jade maintains inner peace during difficult times. Rose Quartz is a stone of infinite compassion and deep peace; it attunes you to unconditional, universal love, and helps you to love yourself. Calcite calms your whole being so that you sink into a deeply peaceful state and attune yourself to unconditional love and stillness.

Rose Quartz

Ammolite

Following the spiral of an Ammolite to its center with your eyes takes you into a place of profound peace and tranquillity. Here, you release anything that troubles you and transmute your fears into infinite peace. Uvarovite Garnet transforms loneliness into an appreciation for solitude and the strength you gain in being alone. Amethyst has long been valued for helping users to still the mind and reach spiritual connection through meditation.

Wear an Amethyst to remind you of your deep well of inner peace. Chrysoprase helps you to feel part of the greater whole and induces a state of deep meditation. If you find it difficult to relax and enter a meditative state, it helps you to let go and feel the divine flow.

Amethyst

CHAKRA SUPPORT SYSTEM Inner peace rests in your heart. Place pink stones over your heart to draw in and anchor deep peace at the center of your being.

SUGGESTED EXERCISES Inner-wealth ritual (pages 68–73), changing your mental blueprint (page 82).

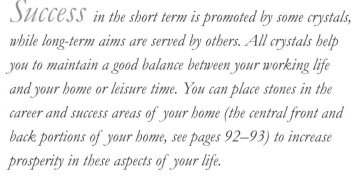

Success *in the short term is promoted by some crystals, while long-term aims are served by others. All crystals help you to maintain a good balance between your working life and your home or leisure time. You can place stones in the career and success areas of your home (the central front and back portions of your home, see pages 92–93) to increase prosperity in these aspects of your life.*

Magnetite

Adamite

Moss Agate

To Attract a New Job

Adamite is useful if you know exactly what job you seek. Place one over the advertisement for a job before you attend an interview. If you cannot find Adamite, use a piece of Iron Pyrite or Magnetite. If you have long-term career plans, magnetize a piece of Tree or other Agate to keep you on track as you work toward your goal. The earthy Tree Agate, or Moss Agate, is appropriate for people who work or want to work outdoors, especially in forestry, agriculture, or horticulture, because it increases fertility of anything that grows. It also enhances your communication with living beings, so it is helpful for veterinary or zoological-associated careers, too.

To Enhance Your Employment Prospects

Invest in some Black Sapphire or Jet jewelry, or put a piece of the darkest blue raw Sapphire you can find by your front door to enhance your employment prospects and to retain a job once you secure it. Cinnabar makes your demeanor elegant and pleasing to the beholder, so it is useful when you want to look your best for jobs in which appearance matters (place it opposite your front door).

Jet

To Help You Study

If you need to pass an examination in order to achieve your goal, Calcite focuses your mind, as does Chalcedony. Sugilite helps you to absorb what you read.

Raw Cinnabar

CHAKRA SUPPORT SYSTEM Stimulate and energize your base chakra with red stones and your throat with blue stones so that you fully communicate your skills and insights to prospective employers.

SUGGESTED EXERCISES Finding the perfect job ritual (pages 86–91).

Crystal Prosperity

Increasing your success depends on how you define success: some people think of success only in terms of money or status, while others think that being happy and fulfilled in life is being successful. Be specific as to whether you want success in the material world, in growing as a person, finding love, meeting your goals, and so on when magnetizing your success stones.

Finding Material Success

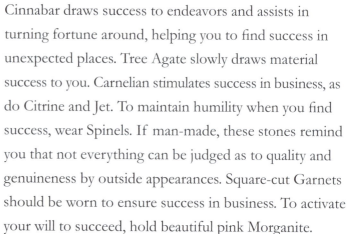

Carnelian

Cinnabar draws success to endeavors and assists in turning fortune around, helping you to find success in unexpected places. Tree Agate slowly draws material success to you. Carnelian stimulates success in business, as do Citrine and Jet. To maintain humility when you find success, wear Spinels. If man-made, these stones remind you that not everything can be judged as to quality and genuineness by outside appearances. Square-cut Garnets should be worn to ensure success in business. To activate your will to succeed, hold beautiful pink Morganite.

Morganite

Finding Creative Success

Aventurine

Aventurine is useful if you are seeking success in creative endeavors, as is Dendritic Agate. This stone of plenitude brings abundance to all areas of life.

Succeeding in Your Goals

If you have specific goals, wear vibrant Topaz, Ruby, Tiger's Eye, or Citrine to bring them to fruition. Hemimorphite helps you to set realistic goals without emotional attachment, while Red Chalcedony encourages persistence in achieving goals.

Successful Love

Wear Emerald to maintain your love and Rose Quartz to enhance your success in love. This stone helps you to fulfill other ambitions, too.

CHAKRA SUPPORT SYSTEM   For material success, stimulate the chakra of the solar plexus with yellow stones, and your sacral chakra with orange ones. For success in love, place appropriate green or pink stones over your heart, and for spiritual success place white, lilac, or pale blue stones over your heart and crown chakras.

SUGGESTED EXERCISES   Gratitude and blessings (pages 46–49), inner-wealth ritual (pages 68–73), asking for blessings on a new venture (pages 94–95), treasure maps (pages 96–97).

109

Achieving My Dreams

Dreams *are a fragile and wondrous thing. We need to distinguish between what is an achievable dream and what is an illusion. Crystals assist in making this distinction. Acting as symbols of what might come into being, crystal eggs nurture and give birth to your dreams. Crystal points draw dreams toward you.*

Bringing Dreams Into Being

Calcite gives courage to act, and courage to be whatever you dream of becoming. It acts as a stepping stone between a dream and its fruition, releasing the limiting beliefs that hold you back. Smoky Quartz manifests dreams and makes them a reality. Jade nurtures your dreams and brings them to fruition. If you need assistance in devising a strategy to make a dream a reality, use Red Chalcedony. Wear Ruby to remain emotionally detached from the outcome.

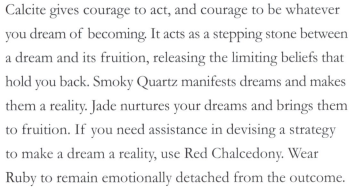

Smoky Quartz

Ruby

Incubating a Dream

If you are not quite sure what you dream of for yourself, magnetize an Aventurine or Moonstone crystal and place it under your pillow. Keep a pen and paper beside the bed to write down your dreams as soon as you wake. Remember that many dreams are symbols of other things.

110

Polished Moonstone

Purple Tourmaline

ABOVE: Crystal eggs detect and correct energy imbalance. They are very useful as comforters that can be held in the hand in times of stress.

Separating an Achievable Dream From an Illusion

Moonstone is an excellent dreaming tool but may induce illusions in sensitive people rather than an achievable reality. Purple Tourmaline or Carnelian strip away illusions and reveal the stark reality behind your dreams. But if the dream is realistic, Carnelian helps it to manifest.

CHAKRA SUPPORT SYSTEM To manifest your dreams, place your crystals over your heart and on the soma chakra at the midpoint of your hairline, above and between your eyebrows (above the third eye). Then place them at your feet to ground your dreams into their physical manifestation.

SUGGESTED EXERCISES Generating money grid (pages 80–85), finding the perfect job ritual (pages 86–91), treasure maps (pages 96–97).

Cosmic *ordering—asking the universe for what you want—is all about being in the flow. Lack of connection to the universal energy source hampers your ability to "go with the flow" and manifest your cosmic order in the material world. Adding crystals to your cosmic order transmutes underlying doubts, self-pity, or fears and amplifies manifestation. Place your crystals on your forehead as you make your order, and also on top of the paper on which you made your order while you await results.*

Green Calcite

Topaz

Bringing a Request to Fruition

Place Green Calcite on your cosmic order to draw riches of all kinds into your home, or magnetize a manifestation crystal (see page 137) to bring you what your heart desires. The positively and negatively charged ends of Topaz send out a request to the universe, which then manifests on the earth.

Believing You Deserve It

Green Calcite is helpful if you have an unconscious underlying belief that you don't deserve to win or to have wealth or prosperity in your life. It gently transmutes the doubt into delighted expectancy.

112

To Release Poverty Consciousness

Citrine and gentle Green Calcite release poverty consciousness and the belief that you don't deserve anything, helping you to move into positive prosperity consciousness.

To Create a Cosmic Energy Flow

Quartz Point

A Quartz point immediately links you with an abundant energy field, as does Aventurine. If you feel miserly because of an inner sense of lack or fear of not being good enough, Citrine transmutes this and plugs you into the abundant flow of energy throughout the universe. To boost your confidence or light your creative spark, hold Iron Pyrite. It quickly ignites your connection to our inexhaustible universal energy flow. Prehnite enhances your trust in the flow of divine manifestation.

Raw Iron Pyrite

CHAKRA SUPPORT SYSTEM Stimulate your soma chakra with appropriate stones, and place silver stones on your earth chakra to ground your dreams into concrete reality.

SUGGESTED EXERCISES Changing the world with intent (pages 52–55), asking for blessings on a new venture (pages 94–95), treasure maps (pages 96–97).

113

Crystal Prosperity

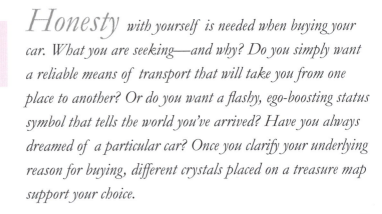

Honesty *with yourself is needed when buying your car. What you are seeking—and why? Do you simply want a reliable means of transport that will take you from one place to another? Or do you want a flashy, ego-boosting status symbol that tells the world you've arrived? Have you always dreamed of a particular car? Once you clarify your underlying reason for buying, different crystals placed on a treasure map support your choice.*

Red Calcite

Buying Your Dream Car

Acting as a stepping stone between a dream and its fruition, Calcite assists a search for something you have longed for. Choose an appropriate color: Red Calcite if it's a flashy status symbol, Black Calcite for a more restrained vehicle. For a romantic dream, choose Mangano Calcite, and for a practical workhorse, Brown Calcite. Smoky Quartz, too, manifests your dreams, and Red Chalcedony devises strategies for successful acquisition.

Black Calcite

Brown Calcite

Buying a Status Symbol

Because Ruby is a stone of wealth and prestige, it assists in finding a car you are passionate about, one that makes you feel really wealthy. Green Aventurine attracts a more conservative status symbol. Chrysoprase helps you to ascertain whether a status-symbol car is merely an ego booster or would bring the recognition you seek.

Buying an Environmentally Friendly Car

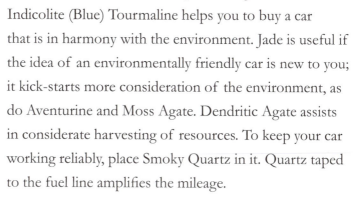

Indicolite (Blue) Tourmaline helps you to buy a car that is in harmony with the environment. Jade is useful if the idea of an environmentally friendly car is new to you; it kick-starts more consideration of the environment, as do Aventurine and Moss Agate. Dendritic Agate assists in considerate harvesting of resources. To keep your car working reliably, place Smoky Quartz in it. Quartz taped to the fuel line amplifies the mileage.

Blue Tourmaline

CHAKRA SUPPORT SYSTEM   For a means of transport from A to B, place brown stones over your earth chakra. For your dream car, place an appropriate stone over your soma chakra first. For a flashy status symbol, place appropriate stones on the base, sacral, and earth chakras.

SUGGESTED EXERCISES   Gratitude and blessings (pages 46–49), charging the world with intent (pages 52–55), generating money grid (pages 80–85).

Crystal Prosperity

Rediscovering lost skills and abilities enriches *you beyond measure, and it's never too late to expand upon an interest or ability you have lost touch with. To find one thing that, even for one brief shining moment, you're better at than anyone else makes you feel special; it enriches you within that moment. But there is enormous pleasure to be found in the process of creating, whatever form it takes. Go back over your life and remember what you enjoyed and what you were good at, no matter how long ago. They may not necessarily be the same and it is by no means essential that they are. You are enriched by doing something simply for the pleasure of doing rather than for the finished result.*

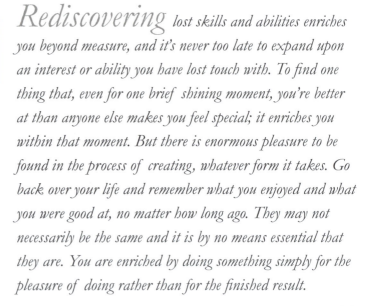

Tumbled Tiger's Eye

Lapis Lazuli

Creativity

Andradite Garnet stimulates creativity and attracts what you most need for your development on all levels. If your creativity has been blocked or simply lost in the mists of time, Tiger's Eye rapidly releases it and helps find a suitable outlet for your creative talents. Wear one to boost your abilities and regain the joy of creation. If it's mental creativity you are seeking, Lapis Lazuli instills clarity and inspiration.

116

Problem Solving and Technology

Topaz sharpens your mind and assists in problem solving, but is also an excellent stone for anyone engaged in the arts. Aventurine assists you in getting to grips with anything technological, enhancing your skills in this area.

Polished Green Aventurine

Storytelling and Active Listening

If you've an interest in storytelling, Pink Chalcedony enhances your skills. This stone instills a sense of childlike wonder and encourages openness to new things. Chinese Writing Stone, or Calligraphy Stone, offers enormous encouragement to writers. People benefit immensely from being listened to in an empathetic way, and Lapis Lazuli has long been valued for enhancing the quality of active listening.

CHAKRA SUPPORT SYSTEM   To discover what you are capable of, place pink crystals over the heart seed chakra at the base of your breastbone, and to regain your power, place appropriate crystals over your sacral chakra.

SUGGESTED EXERCISES   Inner-wealth ritual (pages 68–73).

117

Crystal Prosperity

Embracing work *as a part of your overall life keeps a balance. Crystals assist in feeling there is sufficient time for everything—it is part of living abundantly. Imbalance can arise out of an inability to say no or set boundaries. Bicolored crystals facilitate a better balance between different areas of your life when combined with a visualization technique done before you sleep.*

Lavender Jade

Aventurine

Setting Boundaries

Agate helps you to do only what is necessary and to say no when appropriate. If you need help in setting boundaries and learning how to say no, wear Aventurine jewelry constantly or tape an Aventurine crystal over your spleen. Calcite is useful when you've always been a "yes" person and need to say "no" gently but firmly. Lavender Jade helps to set clear boundaries between yourself and others.

Taking Time Out

If you need time away from work or from the demands of family, Almandine Garnet supports taking time out for yourself; Andradite Garnet gives courage to do whatever is best for you.

118

Turquoise

Merlinite

Bringing About a Balance

At night, put Merlinite under your pillow. Close your eyes and picture an old-fashioned pair of scales with pans on each side hanging from a pivot. On one side, picture something that represents your working life. On the other, something that represents home or leisure time. The pans will come to a stop with one pan higher than the other. Add a Merlinite crystal to the higher one so that the pans become balanced. Ask that in the morning you intuitively know how to find this balance in your life. When you wake, note your dreams or other signals as to how you can rearrange your life. Wear Merlinite to remind you to seek balance, or Turquoise to find creative solutions to balancing your life.

CHAKRA SUPPORT SYSTEM   Place a brown crystal on the earth chakra beneath your feet, an orange crystal on your sacral chakra, a pink stone on your heart, and a blue stone on your soma chakra.

SUGGESTED EXERCISES   Gratitude and blessings (pages 46–49), changing the world with intent (pages 52–55), inner-wealth ritual (pages 68–73).

Relationships of all kinds contribute greatly to your sense of inner wealth. As you align yourself more strongly to your inner resources, so your outer vibrations change and attract into your life people who support your world view.

Place or wear the relevant stones over your heart. A pendant worn on a long chain is particularly suitable for attracting good relationships because it places a suitable crystal over your heart.

Twin Flame

To Attract a Twin Flame

A soulmate or twin-flame crystal has two points springing side by side from the same base. A twin flame is like a soulmate but without the karma. Soulmates can scour our soul; twin flames enrich heart and soul. Wear Blue Aragonite or Turquoise to attract a twin flame who supports your soul's plan and with whom you share deep love and soul-to-soul communication.

Blue Aragonite

To Enhance an Existing Relationship

Rose Quartz is unconditional love. Its presence creates loving harmony. To rekindle love that is feeling stale, wear Morganite because it increases the sense of value in

Rose Quartz

a relationship. If forgiveness would help, Mangano Calcite is perfect. Place one under your pillow to maintain unconditional love and release anything that may be keeping a relationship mired in an unsatisfactory past. If it's more passion you seek, use Ruby, Garnet, Red Jasper, or Green Aventurine.

To Attract New Friends

Chrysoprase encourages fidelity and integrity, teaching that cooperation is more enriching than competition. It attracts like-minded friends who enjoy sharing mutual interests. Jade is the ultimate friendship stone.

Red Jasper

Polished Jade

Merlinite

CHAKRA SUPPORT SYSTEM To enrich a heart connection, place pink or green crystals over your heart. To enrich a mutually supportive and passionate connection, place red crystals over your base chakra and orange crystals below your navel. To increase an emotional connection, place pink or yellow crystals over your solar plexus.

SUGGESTED EXERCISES Gratitude and blessings (pages 46–49), abundance layout (pages 74–79).

121

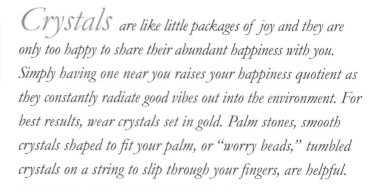

Crystals are like little packages of joy and they are only too happy to share their abundant happiness with you. Simply having one near you raises your happiness quotient as they constantly radiate good vibes out into the environment. For best results, wear crystals set in gold. Palm stones, smooth crystals shaped to fit your palm, or "worry beads," tumbled crystals on a string to slip through your fingers, are helpful.

Crystal Prosperity

Fluorite Palm Stone

Topaz

Cavansite

Joy Bringers

Citrine, Topaz, and Sapphire help you to feel that life is fundamentally joyful. The golden hue of Citrine and Topaz symbolizes the sun; everyone feels more joyful in the sunshine, so wear one of these crystals to lift your spirits. Mellow Orange or Yellow Jade have been used to bring more joy into life for thousands of years and were much prized for their ability to promote happiness. All these crystals increase the flow of endorphins in your brain, as does beautiful sea-blue Cavansite. (Endorphins are natural antidepressants that greatly enhance your feel-good factor.)

Yellow or Golden Calcite instills a quiet joy deep within and facilitates the joy of spiritual connection, as do Stellar Beam Calcite and Chrysoprase. Pink Chalcedony and Mangano Calcite increase joy in your heart. If you

want to enjoy life to the fullest, wear Emeralds or carry
Green Tourmaline.

Optimism

Carnelian

Having an optimistic outlook on life adds to your joy;
wearing Citrine overcomes innate pessimism and instills
hope and optimism. As pessimism only flourishes when
you feel low in energy, wear Carnelian, Citrine, or Topaz
to raise your energy levels and create a positive outlook
on life. These stones transform negativity into joy.

Feeling Positive

Citrine

Whenever you need to feel particularly positive, connect
to Iron Pyrite. The strength in this stone both motivates
and activates you to move into joy.

CHAKRA SUPPORT SYSTEM   Place yellow crystals over
your solar plexus, and green or pink stones over your
heart. If you want to connect to the joy of creativity,
add an orange stone to your sacral chakra.

SUGGESTED EXERCISES   Gratitude and blessings (pages
46–49), inner-wealth ritual (pages 68–73).

123

Chapter 4

The Prosperity Stones Directory

A correspondence between different colored stones and prosperity is an ancient concept. Gold and golden stones have long been associated with wealth, creativity, and the sun that makes things grow, and green stones with the abundance of nature and new growth. Traditionally, gold stones enhance our self-esteem and the feeling that we deserve unlimited abundance, while many red stones are associated with the planet Mars, which symbolizes ambition, the drive to move forward in life, and the willpower to manifest our desires.

Some of the stones in this directory can be found in myriad forms and colors; the basic energy of the stone remains the same, although it may be enhanced by additional properties specific to the variety or color.

Crystal Prosperity

Citrine Known as "the Merchant Stone" and associated with the sun, abundance, and success, Citrine is particularly prized for its prosperity-enhancing properties. It is traditional to keep a Citrine in your purse or in a money box—or the wealth corner of your home—so that it attracts money to you. Keep it in your pocket if you are seeking success. Paradoxically, this stone encourages both generosity and accumulation of wealth. It helps you to freely share joy and abundance, and expand your heart. Citrine teaches that what you give away returns multiplied fourfold, and that generosity of spirit is both a precious gift and a powerful generator of wealth on all levels.

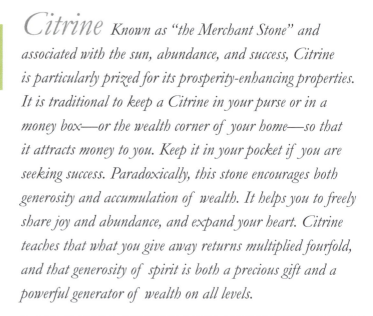

Raw Citrine

If you suffer from a feeling of lack in any part of your life, gazing into the joyful, bright energy of Citrine assists in counting your blessings and raises your self-confidence. This is an excellent stone to use if you lack motivation because it overcomes apathy and hopelessness and raises your self-esteem, promoting optimism and a positive attitude. Citrine is a stone of creativity that helps you to capitalize on your skills and talents; it stimulates your mind to see new possibilities and bring them into form.

Citrine Point

126

Citrine Geode

Polished Citrine

FORMS Citrine is available in various shapes and is ideal for the wealth corner of your home. The cavelike geode helps you to collect and conserve abundance, the many-pointed cluster generates wealth, the single point attracts abundance and brings energy into your physical environment or your body, the sphere radiates energy and prosperity out into the environment, and the tumbled stone reminds you that prosperity is a state of mind.

SOURCE Citrine is a form of Quartz colored by iron impurities. Natural Citrine is comparatively rare; it is created when Amethyst is superheated in the earth's crust. Most Citrine today is artificially formed by heat treatment of Amethyst or Smoky Quartz. Natural Citrine tends to be paler or smokier than the bright yellow or chestnut brown of the artificially heat-amended crystal, but all are effective manifestors of wealth. Natural Citrine is found in the Congo, Brazil, the United States, Britain, Russia, Uruguay, France, and Madagascar.

HISTORY Due to its scarcity in its natural form, Citrine is rarely heard of before the Roman period and was not used for jewelry in the West until the Middle Ages. References to it in early documents and the modern Bible are generally a mistranslation.

Crystal Prosperity

Aventurine Used as a gambler's lucky talisman for centuries, the name Aventurine comes from the Latin for "by chance." Blue and Green Aventurine are often sold as "the abundance stone." Its sparkling flecks made it popular for protective amulets in ancient times and it was often called "Emerald" in countries that did not have access to the more expensive stone. Aventurine makes an excellent gratitude stone because it helps you to value what you already have.

Green Aventurine overcomes the feeling of lack that so often underlies poverty consciousness. It helps you to look forward with joyous expectation to a change in fortune, and provides support if you are going outside your comfort zone. Traditionally, Green Aventurine was used to enhance eyesight; if you need to take a long hard look at yourself or your plans, this stone assists. Aventurine facilitates examining your own motives and behavior; it helps to turn a situation around and assists you in spotting business opportunities that enrich your life in unexpected ways. It increases confidence and brings out leadership qualities, strengthening your integrity and compassion. If you need encouragement to persevere or have a difficult

Raw Blue Aventurine

128

decision to make, keep an Aventurine palm stone in your pocket; if you want to overcome fear, tape Aventurine over your kidneys. Aventurine has strong links with the devic kingdom in which live the plant spirits who oversee Nature; it increases the fertility and abundance of crops, and it enhances gardens and farms. It also enhances your own creativity. Green Aventurine is invaluable if you come under the influence of an energy pirate who drains your energy to top up their own: tape it over your spleen below your left armpit.

Tumbled Green Aventurine

FORMS Opaque and occasionally translucent, Aventurine is a mixture of Feldspar and Quartz with inclusions of Mica or Hematite that add to its sparkling appearance and take a good polish. It can be found in raw chunks, tumbled stones, and shaped pieces. It is available in several colors including blue, green, and soft peach.

Polished Aventurine

SOURCE Aventurine is found in deposits all over the world. It is particularly common in China, India, Tibet, Nepal, Tanzania, Russia, Italy, and Brazil.

HISTORY Prized because of its sparkle, which imitates that of gold or silver, Aventurine was used in the ancient world for statues of the gods. These were looked on as the embodiment of the gods on the earth.

129

Jade *Highly prized in China and the Far East, Jade is the ultimate attractor of good luck and enduring friendship. Its value is equivalent to gold and diamonds. When a Jade nodule is auctioned, the buyer does not know what is inside. It could be excellent quality or almost worthless. The buyer has to take a chance, using intuition or expertise.*

Jade assists you to be grateful for what you have, and to recognize that true riches are not found in the bank but rather within your own self. If you have issues around money, whether you have poverty consciousness or regard money almost as a god, Jade assists. It helps you to regard money positively, valuing what you have and using it wisely. This stone helps you to make the most of what you have and to think laterally in order to bring out hidden riches—or to take a lucky gamble. Linking into the abundance of the universe, it shows how money and precious objects are part of an ongoing energy flow. Releasing ingrained core beliefs and changing your attitude, Jade helps you be self-sufficient and to recognize that the resources you need are already at your disposal. If you seek partners for new ventures, it finds people with integrity and foresight. With Jade's assistance,

Mayan artifact made from raw Jade.

130

previously complex situations become straightforward, and holding serene Blue Jade makes you feel nothing is beyond your control. If you have difficulty setting clear boundaries, wear soft Lavender Jade.

FORMS Jade is actually Jadeite or Nephrite. Jadeite has a soapy feel to it that takes a lustrous glassy polish, and the slightly coarser, more grainy Nephrite is used for carvings and tumbled stones. Jade is available in virtually all colors.

SOURCE Jade is found in China, Italy, the United States, Guatemala, Burma, Russia, and the Far and Middle East.

HISTORY A five-thousand-year-old Jadeite ax head was found recently in England; it appears to have been imported from Italy for ceremonial or ritual purposes. The fact that it had traveled thousands of miles shows how much the stone was valued in the ancient world, especially as it made an excellent cutting tool. Similarly, Jade objects were buried with the emperor and other wealthy citizens of China to indicate status and to pave the way to the next world, where it was believed to offer protection. Jade was used for many ritual objects in the Mayan civilization. It was the sacred greenstone of the Maoris.

Tumbled Jade

Chinese Carved Jade

131

Crystal Prosperity

Carnelian The thirteenth-century Lapidary of King Alphonso *tells us that at one time Carnelian was available only in the remote Yemen, and that only extremely poor and needy men were desperate enough to search for it. For its discovery they were no doubt well rewarded as this stone was much prized in the ancient world for jewelry and as a carving stone. This gives us a clue to the courage with which Carnelian imbues a person set on a difficult course of action, ensuring that a positive end is reached after much struggle.*

Raw Carnelian

The stone was greatly valued for its protective properties and was used throughout the ancient world for amulets of power and protection, and for assuring the wearer of success in commerce. A crystal of creativity, Carnelian has great vitality and is a powerful energizer, especially for the lower chakras. A stone of regeneration, it assists in making positive life choices and in turning daydreams into reality. If you lack motivation or suffer from mental lethargy, this is the stone for you. Carnelian transmutes anger or a sense of victimhood into empowerment and the drive to get things moving. Traditionally, it should be placed in the porch or doorway of a house to invite prosperity to enter your home.

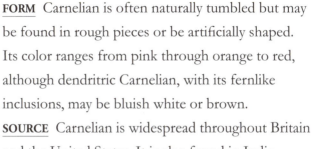

FORM Carnelian is often naturally tumbled but may be found in rough pieces or be artificially shaped. Its color ranges from pink through orange to red, although dendritric Carnelian, with its fernlike inclusions, may be bluish white or brown.

SOURCE Carnelian is widespread throughout Britain and the United States. It is also found in India, Russia, Brazil, central Europe, Peru, and Iceland. It may be found as a water-tumbled stone on beaches or rivers.

Polished Carnelian

HISTORY Highly valued for its ease of carving and translucent beauty, Carnelian jewelry and amulets are found in virtually every ancient civilization across the world. Jewelry made from it has been found in predynastic Egypt, and it occurs in the earliest crystal healing recipes of both Mesopotamia and Egypt. It was almost certainly one of the stones in the breastplate of Aaron, brother of Moses, the Hebrew high priest mentioned in the Bible. In ancient Egypt, highly prized, gem-quality Carnelian from an island in the Red Sea was known as the Blood of Isis (the mother-sister goddess of rebirth and regeneration), and is found on Tutankhamun's funerary jewelry and other artifacts.

Tumbled Carnelian

133

Crystal Prosperity

Ammolite Promoted as the feng shui prosperity stone, Ammolite is a comparatively recent entrant into the crystal market. It has rapidly gained popularity both for its beauty and its powers of attraction and personal empowerment. It stimulates your creativity and stamina, teaching you that perseverance pays off. It is a great stone to keep in the home to promote well-being, and on business premises to ensure success.

Placed over your third eye, Ammolite opens your connection to your spiritual gifts, such as intuition and foresight, and attracts appropriate guides and mentors in the spirit world. When placed over the third eye, it promotes mental clarity and insight. The stone also works well with the base chakra to activate your survival instincts, and when placed on the soma chakra it connects to your soul plan for the present incarnation. Meditating with its spiral takes you deep within yourself, allowing you to recognize and release the ingrained toxic thoughts and emotions that are holding you back from gaining true prosperity. It can also be magnetized to bring a project to fruition.

Mineralized Ammonite

FORM A form of Aragonite often interspersed with Pyrite, Ammolite began life as the shell of a living squidlike creature that became an ammonite fossil; this was compressed and mineralized over millions of years to create a crystal with iridescent flashes of color. The curving shape of the ammonite can still be seen clearly within some Ammolite slices. The spiral is not visible in the small sections used for jewelry.

SOURCE Strictly speaking, Pink Ammolite, a trademarked name, is mined on the eastern slopes of the Rocky Mountains from Alberta, Canada, down to Montana, USA. A similar mineralized fossil can be obtained in parts of Morocco.

HISTORY Ammolite was afforded the status of a biogenic (organic) gemstone only in 1981 by the World Jewellery Confederation. Ammonite has been highly prized throughout history; it was called called "the horn of Amun (the sun god)" in ancient Egypt and it is the amuletic "buffalo stone" of the Blackfoot tribe in the United States.

Polished Ammolite

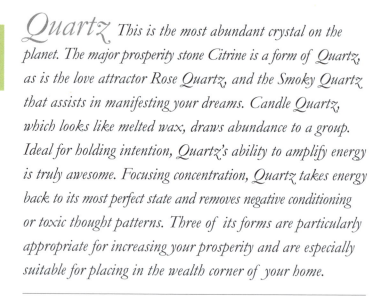

Quartz This is the most abundant crystal on the planet. The major prosperity stone Citrine is a form of *Quartz*, as is the love attractor Rose *Quartz*, and the Smoky *Quartz* that assists in manifesting your dreams. Candle *Quartz*, which looks like melted wax, draws abundance to a group. Ideal for holding intention, *Quartz's* ability to amplify energy is truly awesome. Focusing concentration, *Quartz* takes energy back to its most perfect state and removes negative conditioning or toxic thought patterns. Three of its forms are particularly appropriate for increasing your prosperity and are especially suitable for placing in the wealth corner of your home.

Quartz Generator

Generator Crystals

Generator crystals come in two shapes. A single generator, natural or artificially shaped, has six equal facets meeting in a point at the top; it is often cut so that it stands point facing upward. This shape increases your inner resources. All single generators project energy out and increase your core energy. Small single generator points draw energy in to enhance your prosperity. A generator cluster has long points radiating out in all directions, each of which creates and projects energy. Such a cluster can be magnetized to bring about several outcomes as it puts

Generator Cluster

energy into all your endeavors equally. Use a generator cluster to heal discord within yourself, your family, or a group that is preventing you from living an enriched life.

Manifestation Crystals

A manifestation crystal is a crystal within a crystal: one or more small crystals totally enclosed by a larger crystal. Inclusions or phantoms are sometimes wrongly sold as manifestation crystals. Manifestations are rare but you may find one in a batch of Quartz points. Creative manifestation crystals amplify your thoughts and intentions, and can be magnetized to manifest anything which would enhance your life, such as joy or artistic ability or contact with guides and mentors. However, these crystals can interpret your desires literally. Use these wonderful treasures wisely, after careful contemplation of what you truly intend.

Abundance Crystals

With many small crystals clustering around the base of a large crystal, an abundance crystal is excellent if you want to attract wealth into your home. They attract many other forms of prosperity, too. Magnetize one to bring you good fortune, good friends, and a good life.

Quartz Abundance Crystal

137

Agate

There are several varieties of Agate. All have the property of grounding energy and stabilizing matter, which assists in bringing your prosperity into concrete manifestation. Most Agates work over a long period of time to bring about practical solutions and to help you attune to your core stability. The Agate is a stone of great strength and lends you enormous support. If you need assistance in fully accepting yourself, Agate is your stone. It increases your confidence and your ability to concentrate, facilitating finding inner security.

Tree Agate

TREE AGATE acts slowly to draw material success into your life. With its powerful connection to living things, this is the stone for cultivating inner wealth and for using natural resources ethically. A stone of perseverance, it helps you to feel safe in the most challenging of circumstances.

DENDRITIC AGATE can be similar to Tree Agate in appearance. Known as the stone of plenitude, it brings abundance to all areas of your life, especially to businesses that are connected to nature and natural resources. If you want to enhance the yield of crops, grid it around the area in which they grow. Dendritic Agate facilitates remaining calm and centered during a crisis.

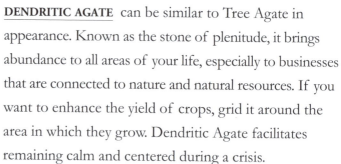

Dendritic Agate

MOSS AGATE also has a profound connection to nature and all that grows. As a birthing crystal, it is extremely useful whenever you are starting a new venture or making a new beginning in your life. Moss Agate is a powerful abundance stone that protects what you have as well as being able to draw inner and outer riches to you. This stone also strengthens your self-esteem. It is the perfect stone if you have lost hope because it promotes trying one more time and also gives you insight into why your efforts have not been successful so far, so that you can amend your plans and achieve success.

SOURCE Agates are found worldwide.

Tumbled Moss Agate

Raw Moss Agate

Emerald

Known as the stone of successful love, Emerald promotes unconditional love and joyful partnership and friendship. It helps you to focus your intention and instills strength to overcome the vicissitudes of life. Whenever you see "Emerald" in the Bible, you can be sure it is a mistranslation of "Green Stone."

SOURCE Tanzania, India, Zimbabwe, Brazil, Austria, and Egypt.

Cut Emeralds

Crystal Prosperity

Tumbled Goldstone

Goldstone

This man-made glass is created by adding copper or other salts to molten glass. Goldstone, in its golden, red, or blue forms, is often sold as "the money stone." It was first designated a gemstone in the nineteenth century, and legend has it that Goldstone was discovered by alchemists as they sought to make gold. Another legend says that it was made in Italy to a secret recipe guarded by a monastic order. It is known that the Miotti family made the stone in seventeenth-century Venice. Today, the stone is valued for its sparkling appearance and its transmutative qualities.

Goldstone instills in the wearer a positive attitude and unshakable self-confidence. It promotes the courage to try something new and enhances energy levels. With the assistance of this sparkling stone, you experience the pleasure of being fully alive and inwardly wealthy.

SOURCE Goldstone is man-made. Pyrite-flecked Sandstone that polishes to look like Goldstone is found in Egypt.

Tiger's Eye

Roman soldiers wore Tiger's Eye amulets to protect them during battle, and it has long been seen as a fortunate stone that protects your resources. Enhancing your ability to make money, Tiger's Eye also imbues the wearer with the ability to accomplish goals and it brings out your assertion skills. This is an excellent stone if you want to make wise use of your own power and draw on inner resources. It assists in recognizing skills and talents, and facilitates change, creating opportunities. If you have been suffering from blocked creativity, Tiger's Eye releases the blockage. It is a useful stone for gathering together disparate pieces of information and synthesizing them into a coherent whole. It also assists in separating what you think you want from what you really need, and recognizing the right moment for action. Distinguishing wishful thinking from attainable possibilities, it strengthens your self-confidence and your commitment.

Raw Tiger's Eye

Golden Tiger's Eye helps you to act from intuition rather than emotion, and Red Tiger's Eye is particularly useful if you lack motivation. Hawk's Eye, another form of Tiger's Eye, dissolves negative thought patterns and helps you to take responsibility for yourself. It is traditionally placed in the wealth corner of a house or business to attract abundance.

SOURCE India, the United States, Mexico, South Africa, and Australia.

Tumbled Tiger's Eye

Crystal Prosperity

Iron Pyrite

Also known as "Fools Gold," Iron Pyrite is an exceptionally strong and fast-acting "macho" stone that gets things moving. In Greek times, it was known as "stone that strikes fire," and it ignites your own creative spark. If you need help to see what lies beneath a facade, call on Iron Pyrite, and also use it if you want to tap into your own potential or to boost your self-confidence.

Raw Iron Pyrite

Iron Pyrite is useful in business because it energizes projects—although it can be too strong if there are "macho men" around. It works best for women and gentle men, instilling stamina and insight within a spirit of mutual cooperation. Use it as a paperweight on a desk to keep ideas flowing. An Iron-Pyrite-in-Quartz stone is the best energetic combination of all for manifestation. **SOURCE** Iron Pyrite is found in Britain, Chile, Peru, and North America.

Polished Lapis Lazuli

Lapis Lazuli

Valued by the ancients as a prosperity stone because of the golden flecks running through it, Lapis Lazuli was seen as the gods made flesh, the sky come down to earth. Instilling self-awareness and serenity, it teaches you the

142

power of the spoken word and heightens creativity. A thought amplifier, it teaches the value of active listening. **SOURCE** Afghanistan, Middle East, the United States, Russia, Chile, Italy, and Egypt.

Turquoise

Sacred to the Egyptian goddess Hathor, the blue-green color of Turquoise was synonymous with joy and vibrant life. Mined in Egypt more than five-and-a-half thousand years ago, the oldest beads in the world, which were Turquoise, were found in Mesopotamia. Believed to unite the earth and the sky, it symbolizes masculine and feminine energy coming into balance. If you need a creative solution to problems, look to Turquoise. If you sabotage yourself just when you're achieving all you've dreamed of, wear Turquoise. This gentle stone quietly strengthens your belief in yourself and projects it into the future. American Indians believed that seeing Turquoise and the new moon together generated wealth, so if you want to attract good fortune with Turquoise, perform your rituals at new moon. **SOURCE** Turquoise is found in Afghanistan, the United States, Egypt, Tibet, Russia, Iran, China, Peru, France, Arabia, and Poland.

Tumbled Turquoise

143

Crystal Prosperity

Raw Topaz

Topaz

Wearing zingy Topaz makes you feel rich in all ways. Helping you to tap into your inner riches, it assists with achieving your goals and finding solutions to problems. Instilling trust in the universe, it helps you to be rather than do. One of the traditional stones of good fortune, this vibrant crystal is imbued with joy and abundance. Helping you to be philanthropic and generous, it assists you in sharing your resources and spreading happiness. Excellent for all creative pursuits, Topaz boosts your confidence and encourages lateral thinking when solving problems.

Blue Topaz helps you to live with integrity in accordance with your own mores and aspirations. If you have strayed from your own truth, it gently points the way back. Golden Topaz is one of the most energetic forms of Topaz. Acting like a battery, it recharges your energies and your optimism. It assists in recognizing your own abilities, and enhances your charisma. If you have great plans, Topaz is perfect to facilitate manifesting them. Pink Topaz dissolves any resistance you may have to letting go of old patterns.

SOURCE Topaz is found in the United States, India, Mexico, South Africa, Australia, Sri Lanka, and Pakistan.

Cut Blue Topaz

Raw Cinnabar

It was first used to provide color for ancient cave paintings, many of which are believed to be part of rituals to ensure success in a hunt. Placed in a cash box, the stone was believed both to draw in wealth and to enable you to hold onto what you had. This is a stone for successful financial dealings. It was said to enhance a seller's powers of persuasion, to make you more assertive, and to bring success in all your endeavors. If you want to make your persona more pleasing, keep Cinnabar near to you as you work the transformation.

SOURCE Cinnabar is found in the United States and China.

CAUTION Cinnabar is a toxic stone, so handle it with care and wash your hands after use.

Adamite

Adamite

This is an unusual stone that may be difficult to acquire, but is worth searching out. It enhances your creativity and assists you in attracting exactly the right job. It helps you to make difficult career choices and find new directions, and it activates your entrepreneurial skills. This stone grows a new business and brings prosperity of all kinds.

SOURCE Adamite is found in the United States, Mexico, and Greece.

Crystal Prosperity

Tumbled Blue Chalcedony

Chalcedony Geode

Chalcedony

A gentle nurturing stone, Chalcedony fosters generosity and benevolence. If you need to release toxic thoughts, Chalcedony transmutes them into joy. It is available in several colors, but not all Chalcedonies are natural, particularly the silver forms, which are painted and wash off. Blue Chalcedony promotes creativity and promulgation of new ideas. It helps you to adjust optimistically to new situations and make the best of them. Energetic Red Chalcedony endows you with confidence and persistence when striving to reach your goals. This stone is most useful for devising strategies that manifest your dreams. <u>SOURCE</u> Chalcedony is found worldwide.

Spinel

Most Spinels are tiny and held on a matrix or set in jewelry. Some of these stones are artificially created, but even these can be magnetized to act in the same way as a natural Spinel by asking that the crystal attune to the spirit of the stone. Spinel helps you overcome misfortune and renews your energy in difficult situations. Spinel is a particularly helpful stone for keeping your ego in check and maintaining

Raw Spinel

humility whenever you achieve success. It never lets you forget where you have come from and those who helped you on your way. Black Spinel assists you to work through your material problems, while Orange Spinel stimulates your creativity. Yellow Spinel enhances your personal power.

SOURCE Canada, Sri Lanka, India, Burma, or man-made.

Tourmaline

A strongly protective stone, Tourmaline removes victim consciousness and instills self-confidence in its place. While all the Tourmalines attract prosperity, Indicolite (Blue) Tourmaline is particularly useful for sharing your inner resources with others in an act of service and for living in harmony with the environment.

Black Tourmaline

Pink Tourmaline attracts a wealth of love, while Purple Tourmaline sweeps away illusions and helps you to have realistic dreams. Encouraging service to others, Paraiba Tourmaline promotes forgiveness and removes self-defeating patterns.

SOURCE Tourmaline is found in Sri Lanka, Afghanistan, the United States, Brazil, Western Australia, Italy, and throughout Africa.

Purple Tourmaline

149

Minor Crystals

Crystal Prosperity

Raw Garnet

Polished Garnet

Tumbled Green
Grossular Garnet

Garnet

This is a powerfully energizing stone that brings you passion or serenity as appropriate. One of the most plentiful crystals, it has long been valued for its ability to enhance sexual potency. Square-cut Garnets are said to ensure success in business. This is an excellent stone to keep with you in a challenging situation that is seemingly hopeless. It strengthens your survival instinct, instills fortitude, and turns a crisis into an opportunity. Garnet assists you to release outdated ideas and plan for the future. Different types and colors of Garnet have different effects. Almandine Garnet supports you in taking time out for yourself, and Andradite Garnet stimulates your creativity and instills courage.

Natural Hexagonal Green Grossular Garnet is an excellent stone for manifestation. This crystal teaches how to go with the flow and inspires you to give service to your fellow human beings. Use Uvarovite Garnet if you want to promote your individuality without falling into the trap of egocentricity. It helps you to value solitude.

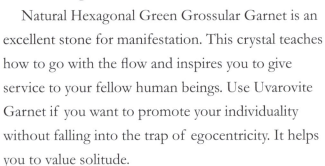

SOURCE Garnet is found throughout the world.

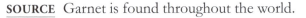

150

Raw Ruby

Polished Ruby

Raw Sapphire

Ruby

This gem has long been prized for its vigor and passion in addition to its ability to attract—and retain—wealth. It is a powerful symbol of status. Strengthening motivation and instilling passion for life, it helps you to set realistic goals, and offers the courage to bring your dreams to fruition. If you want to enhance your individuality while at the same time retaining your connection to those around you, wear Ruby in Zoisite (Anyolite).

SOURCE Rubies are found in Sri Lanka, Russia, India, Madagascar, Mexico, Cambodia, and Kenya.

Sapphire

A joyful Sapphire brings an influx of prosperity into your life as money or other resources. Each color of Sapphire has its own particular properties. Wear Black Sapphire to enhance your employment prospects or to retain your job in challenging times. Use Pink Sapphire as a magnet to draw into your life everything you need for growth and self-development. Traditionally, a Yellow Sapphire in your money box is said to keep the money rolling in.

SOURCE Sapphires are found in Sri Lanka, Burma, Czech Republic, Brazil, India, Kenya, and Australia.

Raw Peridot

Tumbled Peridot

Tumbled Merlinite

Peridot

Regarded as a powerfully protective stone in ancient times, Peridot may have been one of the stones in the breastplate of the Hebrew High Priest. A stone of financial and spiritual abundance, it releases the negative beliefs and the toxic thought patterns and feelings that underlie poverty consciousness. Instilling confidence in your own abilities, Peridot assists in seeing the gifts in your past, including mistakes that were learning experiences. It is a useful stone for bringing about change, especially one based on recognition of your own inner resources. Peridot helps you to leave behind your old habits, such as spending too much or being miserly. Overcoming jealousy, it assists in putting out to the universe the message that you are ready to accept abundance right now. SOURCE Peridot is found in the United States, Russia, Brazil, Ireland, Sri Lanka, Egypt, and the Canary Islands.

Merlinite (Psilomane)

This stone attracts good fortune into your life and has a touch of magic about it. Wear it when you want to pull off something unusual or unexpected that needs luck and serendipity. Perfect for bringing balance between complementary or opposing forces, Merlinite turns a negative experience into a positive learning situation.

SOURCE Merlinite is found in New Mexico.

Moonstone

A stone of new beginnings and intuitive understanding, Moonstone helps you to work with cycles and flows, tuning into exactly the right moment for action or nonaction. Feminine in nature, it draws out old emotional patterning that restricts you, but it can also make you overly emotional at full moon. It is perfect for new moon rituals. Blue Moonstone enables you to keep a foot in both worlds: the spiritual and the material.

Polished Moonstone

SOURCE It is is found in Sri Lanka, Australia, and India.

Blue Aragonite

The energy and the color of Blue Aragonite derive from copper. A highly optimistic stone, it assists you in turning problems and crises into opportunities. This stone helps you to access your soul's plan for the present life.

SOURCE Blue Aragonite is found in the United States, Britain, Namibia, Spain, and Morocco. Its color may be artificially enhanced.

Blue Aragonite

Crystal Prosperity

Refer to pages 80–85 for the Generating Money Grid instructions and Chapter 3 to use the Chakra Support System opposite.

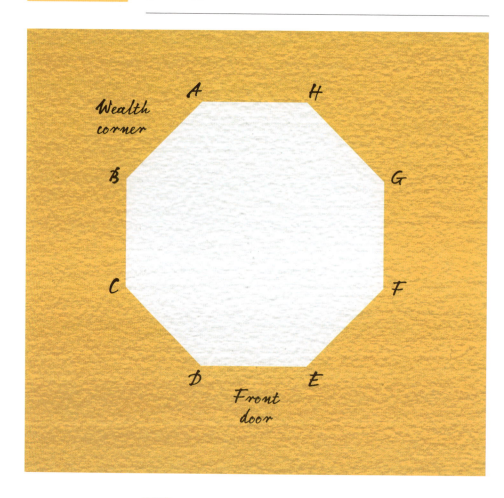

Wealth corner

A   H

B   G

C   F

D   E

Front door